Behind the Smile

HEALING FROM ABUSE, TRAUMA, AND BETRAYAL

JOHN STERNFELS, LPC
MELISSA ROBERTS

Fulton Books
Meadville, PA

Published by Fulton Books 2024

ISBN 979-8-88982-852-5 (paperback)
ISBN 979-8-89221-404-9 (hardcover)
ISBN 979-8-88982-853-2 (digital)

Printed in the United States of America

Behind every beautiful smile is a bitter sadness, which no one ever gets to see or hear.

—Unknown

CONTENTS

INTRODUCTION

As a little girl, I dreamed of what my life would look like when I grew up and what I would do, where I would live, whom I would marry, and how many children I would have. I even dreamed about what kind of dog I wanted. My dream life would be perfect in every way.

Although my dreams varied throughout my younger life, I knew one thing that would not change: I would not accept a life filled with anger, rage, abuse, fear, or loneliness. Instead, my life was to grow in love, safety, peace, and connection—much different than what I experienced as a child.

I would often dream about becoming an elementary school teacher. I envisioned a classroom filled with happy, smiling faces, and everyone would be excited to see me. Every morning, the children would shout, "Good morning, Ms. Turner!"

The classroom walls would be lined with the students' academic accomplishments and their creative artwork. Large block alphabet letters from *A* to *Z* would outline the tops of the walls, about four feet from the ceiling. Additionally, I envisioned numerals from 1 to 10 taped just below the alphabet letters. Anyone could easily see and read these as they walked by my room.

I imagined pictures of exotic animals from Africa, India, and the North Pole. Stars and planets in magnificent colors would hang from the ceiling. I would have an exceptional classroom indeed. My classroom would be my happy place to experience unyielding value and respect—a place where I was loved and appreciated, a place where my smile would be honest and genuine.

I dreamed of marrying a happy, fun-loving man who deeply loved our children and me. He would be active in our church, cherish serving alongside me, and display a gracious heart.

My dream husband would love the Lord with all his heart, and he would be mature in knowing what true love was and how to provide it to me. Most of all, my dream marriage was being one with God.

I dreamed about living in a two-story house with vinyl and brick siding. It would be surrounded with trees and have a backyard big enough to watch the children play as our dog ran back and forth. We would have a swing set and a place where our kids could entertain other children from the neighborhood. Love and laughter would fill the air.

Lastly, we would have a section in the yard where I would get my fingers dirty in the warm spring soil, planting and caring for the most colorful flowers throughout the seasons.

Our front yard would be the envy of the neighborhood, with lush, weed-free grass and manicured green shrubs for year-round enjoyment. We would spend time on the front porch at night, sitting in rocking chairs, enjoying each other with laughter and song.

What did come true was that I became a mother to two wonderful children. Although I did not want them to grow up in a dysfunctional home, they did. Although I did not want my children to live with divorced parents, they did. Although I did not want my children to have an absent father, they did. Although I did not want my children to experience a mother who had to hide her sadness behind her smile, they did. One of my biggest regrets is allowing my children to live in a home filled with instability, hurt, pain, and loneliness.

What did not come true was that I did not become a schoolteacher; instead, I became a paraprofessional at the local elementary school. My area of responsibility included implementing a reading program (with the help of many volunteers) and matching each student's needs to the volunteer's skill set. I was also responsible for the school crossing guard duties, assisting in the library, and working in small classroom groups to help with students' reading skills.

Teachers and schoolchildren would call me Ms. Turner, the "teacher" who always smiled. I perfected my smile and laughter to hide the pain on the inside.

On the outside, I learned to minimize my fear, hurt, and loneliness. I hid the pain very well, almost too well, I would say. I carried the pain at home and in public.

What everyone saw was my happy and friendly face. I thought this was how life was, one part of me feeling pain and hurt and the other projecting joy and happiness. After all, that is what I learned growing up—to live life *behind a smile*.

My story begins by sharing my turbulent and abusive home-life growing up. Many experiences left me with numerous scars that affected much of my life. Most of my healthy decision-making abilities never took root. I learned very well to carry my deeply stored anger within me, unwilling to acknowledge or confront it.

I never knew how to acquire the emotional bandwidth necessary to address or deal with it, so I learned very early to pack it deep down and keep it inside me, never to be seen or shared with anyone.

One of the earliest teachings I learned was, if I let my unpleasant feelings (such as anger, disappointment, or hurt) be known, I would experience extreme disapproval from my father. He had little to no tolerance for emotions from either himself or others.

Sharing my feelings was like living in a paradox: damned if you do, and damned if you don't. I learned to either hold them in and experience internal emotional instability or take a chance and let my feelings be known and reap the consequences.

The consequences of sharing my feelings resulted in extreme punishment. With only two options, I learned it was better to keep my emotions locked inside me for fear of disapproval.

Early in life, I promised never to look or act like my angry, alcoholic father. Due to the abuse I experienced growing up, I developed severe bladder control issues and low self-esteem. I believed I was unlovable and did not belong to anyone or anything, including God.

As a young teenager, I remember reading books about how my life would likely turn out, marrying a man just like my dad or developing an addiction myself. I remember reading about how addictions are hereditary and are encoded in our DNA. This scared me as I did not want to marry anyone like my dad or develop an addiction.

I intentionally married a man who was just the opposite of my father. I married an extremely passive man, a nondrinker, and one who seemed to love the Lord.

My story is indeed a God story. The pages contain my personal story of healing from sexual, emotional, mental, physical, and spiritual abuse. As if that were not enough, my healing journey includes having to heal from being a partner to a sex addict. With all the safeguards in place, I never thought I would marry any sort of addict. My dream was to live free of addiction, abuse, and pain. Time and time again, I would tell myself, "This is not how it was supposed to be."

Looking back, I can see where I turned my back on God, believing he should have known what I went through and should have protected me from everything I experienced. With twenty-twenty hindsight, I can now see that God was always present and did not abandon or forsake me through any part of my life. God showed me how he and only he would turn my mess into his message, a test into a testimony, a trial into a triumph, and a victim into a victory!

I am so excited that you have chosen to read this book. I want you to know how my early childhood experiences influenced many adult decisions, thoughts, and reactions.

As you know, life presents difficulties and sometimes inexcusable and excruciating pain. However, I want you to know that God is still there with you, regardless of what you may be going through. He was with me, even though I turned my back on him.

If you experience a trigger at any point in this book, it is okay to skip that part and read ahead. You can always choose to come back to it later. I pray that you can see that no life circumstance is too impossible for God to work through and heal. Like me, God can help you through any situation or circumstance, no matter how awful. God can take you from victim to victor.

I have learned the importance of obedience and surrender. Focusing on God in all circumstances gave me a perspective I would have never known. God's perspective is always right.

What you are about to read is true. My story is messy—there is no sugarcoating—and I admit it was not easy to write. Whatever you may be going through, I pray that God shows you what he showed me: that he cares and loves me like no one ever could or will. Looking back, I can see how God never gave up on me, no matter what I experienced.

I want to leave you with this important reminder:

> God's perspective is vital to understand painful or difficult circumstances we experience. When facing hardships or confusing situations, they can overwhelm us. When we look at God from the middle of the circumstance, we will always have a distorted under-standing of Him.—(Henry T. Blackaby, *Experiencing God: Knowing and Doing the Will of God*)

SECTION I
Behind the Smile

CHAPTER 1

The Early Years

I am living proof that no matter what we go through in life...we all have the strength to get through it and past it, if we allow ourselves to.

—Barbra Green

My father was a handsome man whom I admired and feared at the same time. I loved the smell of the Old Spice cologne he put on every time he went out. Today, it is still one of my favorite men's colognes.

He was also a complex man. At times, he would be fun-loving and in great spirits, while at other times, he would be the meanest SOB you could imagine. His laughter and jokes would light up any room, though his fun-loving side was the one I rarely experienced.

He seemed to have the gift of fixing anything that broke (except his life). Even as an adult, I would not hesitate to ask him how to fix something that needed repairing rather than replacing. Sadly, behind this fun, gifted, handsome man was a man haunted by a dark side he would never talk about. He had deep emotional pain that spilled into the lives of everyone around him.

My parents grew up on the same country dirt road in Southern Indiana. In my early years, I was not aware that my father had grown up in a dysfunctional family home. He was the only child of his mother but one of eleven on his father's side. I learned that my paternal grandfather had married and divorced five times, having nearly a dozen children conceived from various marriages.

My father's parents divorced when he was eight, leaving him alone with his mother. My grandfather had an abusive nature and a secret alcohol addiction.

Having plenty of time alone, he had endless freedom to roam the neighborhood and be mischievous. His mother had her own issues: I learned later she had attempted suicide to attempt to end her pain.

I never knew much about my mother's side of the family. However, I learned later in life that her family, too, struggled with alcoholism. Furthermore, I learned that my mother had conceived two other children by two men other than my father. I also became aware that before marrying my father, my mother gave her first child up for adoption but chose to keep her second child, a baby girl.

Even though my father knew of my mother's prior pregnancies, they married at twenty-four. I discovered my mother was already pregnant with a boy, my older biological brother.

Unfortunately, I also found out my father never really liked the little girl my mother had before marrying him. Shortly after their marriage, my father sent my half sister to live at my maternal grandmother's home. As far as I know, there was no discussion or compromise. To keep the peace, my mother had to give her daughter to her mother to raise.

Not long after, my mother became pregnant again. She had another baby girl—me! I was the second oldest of four children. A few years later, I would be a sister to two more siblings.

When I was in my teens, my mother informed me that my younger siblings all resulted from a night of drunkenness. They had only wanted two children. As a result, it became permanently etched in my mind that even though I was the second child (excluding my older half sister), I was the result of a drunken sexual encounter. That left me feeling unwanted, hopeless, and unworthy of love.

My father worked full-time at a factory, although I do not remember what his position was. I remember hearing stories of him passing out, which caused apparent concerns for my mother. As a result, my father was sent to the doctor's office, though the test results showed nothing physically wrong. I believe it was my mother who then had him see a psychiatrist, who put him on a powerful medication my father always referred to as his "nerve" pills.

After seeing his psychiatrist for a time, my father quit his factory job and became a stay-at-home dad. This all occurred in the 1960s, when a stay-at-home dad was not customary.

Soon after, I realized that my father had agoraphobia (fear of going out in public). I remember him staying at home, taking care of the cooking and yard work, caring for the chickens we raised, and tending to the backyard garden—both of which were necessary due to my parents' lack of income. Interestingly, my father had enough money to pay for his drinks at the bar but not enough to take care of his family.

My father's responsibility for my siblings and me was not the greatest. I remember he would have my mother do the grocery shopping so he could go to the local bars to drink. He would return when the sun went down, just before dinner. You could say he was well-known by the bar owners.

My father's routine eventually ended after my mother's health issues forced him to attend to "some" of the family's needs.

As backward as this may seem, I grew resentful of my mother over her poor health and for causing my father to take on more at home, even though my father was the abuser. I guess I craved his approval and acceptance and feared that I, too, would be sent to live with my grandmother.

Even though my mother tried to protect and defend us against my father's anger and abuse, we turned against her. Dad told us to call our mother the "Old Lady" instead of "Mother." I cannot imagine what he would have done if we had called her "Mother."

My father often told us that the "Old Lady" was scum because she had two other children by two different men. As I previously mentioned, he harbored resentment over her two prior pregnancies, and we joined him in his negativity.

I never knew my mother's side of the family because my father seldom allowed us to visit them. My guess is, it was because my

5

grandmother was raising my half sister, whom my father wanted nothing to do with. Because of my father's brainwashing and abusive ways, I resented my mother for never removing us from a harsh and dangerous life. My mother was too scared to fight him because he ruled with an abusive fist.

COUNTRY LIVING

As young children, we lived in a two-story farmhouse in the country. My earliest memory was when my father became furious when I had difficulty pedaling my tricycle! I still remember how big, intimidating, and scary he looked as I tried with all my might to push the pedals of my trike with no result. All I wanted was for my father to be proud of me. When I was three, I remember being fragile, small, and uncoordinated, which I still am today. Having my father's approval was important to me at a very young age.

Occasionally, my father would take us kids to the bar, which we did not look forward to. We were ordered to sit very still, or there would be severe punishment. Frightened to no end, we would watch our father sit back and enjoy a few bottles of beer with his drinking buddies, unaware of how much time slipped by in that smelly, scary bar.

As if that was not enough to scare us, there were many times when my mother and father would be in a heated discussion over my father's drinking. One night, when we were tucked safely away in our beds, we heard a terrifying scream. My mother rushed into our bedroom, grabbed us and our belongings, and hurried us out of the house as fast as possible.

We ran down the hill in our backyard to our picnic table and were told to hide so our father would not hurt us. My sibling and I were terrified. This was the only time our mother physically removed us from the house, fearing our father's violent ways.

My Pet Name

I was the only child with a nickname bestowed by my father. I must admit I was highly flattered but a little confused at the same time. As I think about it, I don't recall my father ever calling me by my real name, Melissa.

My father's nickname for me was Imp. It would stay with me even into my adulthood. I learned later that my father had chosen that name because he saw me as a "mischievous child," which always puzzled me. I saw myself as the most compliant child of the four of us. Even today, I tend to be known as a people pleaser and compliant to everyone.

I never liked rocking the proverbial boat because it always resulted in severe consequences. If my father did not call me Imp, he would call me Pinhead. I guess I had two nicknames.

I learned to accept these names as terms of endearment since he had no special names for my siblings. Although I was not fond of these names and was publicly embarrassed, I never said anything to him for fear of being disciplined.

I realize now that thinking of these demeaning names as terms of endearment was warped, but I learned at a very early age to find the best way to cope with confusing and fearful situations.

Moving to the Suburbs

When I was four, due to financial issues, we moved from our spacious country home to a tiny two-bedroom house in the suburbs. My mother worked as a secretary for minimum wage, which was the only household income at the time.

Most of my memories began there in that house. As an adult, I learned that our household differed from most households. I remember thinking our way of life was "normal."

When my siblings and I were little, we were always made to sit still in one specific spot and instructed not to move, or else there would be severe punishment. At times, we were forced to sit for hours. It was my father's way of keeping us controlled and contained.

My younger brother was no exception. He was also taught at an early age to sit still in his high chair throughout the day—this lasted until he was five or six years of age.

When he grew too big for the high chair, my father would tie him to a child's chair-and-table set with a couple of small toys to play with for the entire day. It would be his spot for many years to come.

My brother could never play with us or explore the outdoors like other children. Recalling his abusive experience with our father breaks my heart. For most of my childhood, this is how I remember him.

As siblings, we were not allowed to play with one another. We were purposely kept apart most of the time. We were not allowed to have any conversations because my father did not like noise or chaos unless it was of his making.

As a result, one of us stayed in the living room watching television, one of us sat at the dinner table with one toy or the Sears catalog, and one stayed outside until our father came home.

Other times, to help keep us separate throughout the day, my sister would be tied to a chair in our oversize laundry room. Although it seemed odd then, I was told it was necessary because we needed to be controlled and contained while our father was at work. I assumed this was what his parents did. Watching my sister tied up throughout the day and left alone like my younger brother was heartbreaking.

We were taught early on never to speak up without permission. We all learned quickly that we did not want to upset our father.

We were never free to use the bathroom unless we asked for permission. Nor were we allowed any freedom to have snacks or a drink of water between meals.

Each of us knew not to get caught violating our father's rules because of the punishment that would follow: severe spankings and additional frightening consequences. My siblings and I were acutely aware of this, especially when my father returned home after drinking with his buddies at the bar.

We were only allowed half a cup of water during and after our meals. I often was denied water because I did not eat fast enough or wet the bed the night before.

Another moment I would never forget was, when we were very thirsty, we would go into the bathroom, flush the toilet, and turn on the faucet, pretending to wash our hands. In reality, we were sneaking a drink of water. Another way we would get water was when we were outside; we would sneak around the house to the garden hose, turn it on very slowly (being careful not to leave a puddle), and take a drink of water. Of course, if we were caught, we were punished for being disobedient.

One evening my father ordered me to go to bed early. My usual routine was to use the bathroom before bed, and I took this opportunity to sneak a drink from the faucet. Unfortunately, I was caught and sent directly to bed. I lay in bed and cried, not understanding the big deal of getting a little water before bed.

NOWHERE TO RUN

Often, my father would have me sit on the living room floor with a Sears catalog to look at for the entire day. I would daydream about escaping my confusing, harsh, and challenging homelife. With the catalog in front of me, I would spend time flipping through each page, dreaming of my future. This included what my home would look like, my clothes, and my children's smiling faces.

On other occasions, I sat in front of the television imagining my life as part of the *Brady Bunch* or *The Waltons*. I noticed that the children in those families had much more freedom than my siblings and I had. They did not experience the kind of punishment we faced if they made a mistake or broke a "rule." They seemed to get along, respected one another, and enjoyed one another's company. There were conversations with their parents, many hugs, and they were loved even when they made wrong choices. I was slowly becoming more aware of the abuse in my household.

Watching commercials on television exposed me to a variety of foods and drinks I never experienced. Of course, I knew these were forbidden, and I remember wishing they would appear when I was hungry or thirsty.

Other times, I would daydream about fainting or being sick so I could find out what it was like to receive positive attention. As hard as I tried to escape into my imagination, life remained harsh and unbearable most of the time.

BIRTHDAYS AND RELATIVES

Birthdays were usually fun growing up, and we looked forward to a break from our mundane life. I remember thinking I would finally be with my siblings and looking forward to eating cake and ice cream.

My paternal grandmother and grandfather would come over with gifts and a beautiful, decorated cake. Our instructions were to look and act as "happy" as possible when they arrived. Ironically, we were allowed to play outdoors and would have more freedom than usual. Our maternal grandparents were never invited to celebrate birthdays with us because our father disliked them.

Birthday celebrations were for family only. We were not allowed to invite our friends. My father never wanted strangers inside our home. Gifts were either a toy or an item from our birthday wish list.

The celebration depended on whether our father was in a good or a bad mood. We could play and enjoy eating ice cream and cake if he were in a good mood. If not, there would be nothing. It was just another day.

My siblings and I looked forward to my father taking one of us to visit our paternal grandmother. My grandmother would have Hershey's candy bars in her refrigerator waiting for us. How exciting it was when we were allowed to enjoy this rare treat, along with a small glass of pop.

My father would plan a family picnic day trip to a local park on a river every year. Although it was a time when most kids would run and play, my father prohibited any running or playing. Instead, it was time for us simply to be out of the house.

Being out of the house was fun because we could cook hot dogs on the grill and roast marshmallows. We always looked forward to this trip because it was a time to laugh and be together, even though we could not run and play.

Because gas was less than thirty cents a gallon, our parents could afford to take us on a Sunday afternoon drive. Of course, we had to sit still for the one-to-two-hour drive, but it was nice to see many new things. It was also a welcome break from sitting and watching television, thumbing through a Sears catalog, or playing outside alone.

CHRISTMASTIME

Christmas holidays came with mixed experiences. Some came with excitement, while others were filled with fear and sadness.

When we were young, my paternal grandmother and her cousin would visit us at Christmas and bring us unexpected gifts. When my grandmother's health issues became a problem, she was no longer invited to spend Christmas with us. It left me wondering if her health issues were contagious or if the drive was too hard for her. I guess I will never know the real reason.

Over the years, my father created a new Christmas tradition. Before we could open any gifts, he would visit the bars, see his friends, and wish them a Merry Christmas. I remember eagerly awaiting his return so we could open our presents. It was typical, however, for my father to find some trivial matter to be angry over, which would eliminate any festive celebration.

An example of a trivial matter would be how one of us would look at him or how my father would become enraged over a towel my mom was using. Yelling and screaming always followed.

My father's drinking never changed. Christmases were powder kegs that incited his rage. He would throw gifts across the living room or heave the Christmas tree, breaking the lights and ornaments. Christmas celebrations were rarely fond memories for us. We were nothing like *The Waltons*.

Bed-Wetting

Many children struggle at one time or another with bed-wetting. I was no different. However, my bed-wetting struggles lasted throughout my childhood, which my father did not know how to handle. As an adult, I learned that my father struggled with bed-wetting in his early adulthood. It made me wonder if he were treated the way he treated me. On the other hand, why was he not more caring and sensitive if he had experienced such treatment? I guess I expected more than he was able to give.

My father would try numerous ways to remedy my problem. If I wanted a blanket in winter, I could not wet the bed in the unheated bedroom. When I did wet the bed, the blanket was taken away from me. Given I could not control wetting the bed, I was left to sleep most nights without a blanket.

My father's attempts to keep me from wetting the bed did not work. My older brother and I shared a bedroom with a set of bunk beds—he slept on the top. On cold nights, my brother would drape half of his blanket onto the bottom bunk so I could have some warmth. My brother was very kind and had to remember to pull his blanket up before anyone entered the room so he would not be punished for helping me.

On weekends, my father occasionally came into the bedroom to check if I had wet the bed, which I did most of the time. As a result, he would yank on my feet to drag my body downward, leaving my face in the urine-soaked sheets.

If I moved, I would be threatened with a spanking. I would have to lie in the urine-soaked sheets for hours until my father said it was okay to get up. It also meant I would have to wear my urine-soaked underwear all day, and it would not take long to develop excruciating sores on my bottom. Of course, this added more to my already offensive body odor.

As a result, it intensified the emotional pain I was experiencing. It also added to my bundle of nerves, making it difficult to fall asleep. Each night, when it was time to go to bed, I feared I would wake up the following day in urine-soaked underpants and would have to wear them again for the entire day.

On very frigid school mornings, my father would send me outside to wait for the bus while he drove my siblings to school. I never understood why I could not be driven to school also.

While waiting for the school bus, I was instructed to stand still and not walk around. My father told me he would monitor my movement and threatened that I would be punished if I did not obey. My father's punishment would be unbearable beatings, especially if I had wet the bed the previous night.

I remember the loneliness of standing outside in the cold wearing my soaked underwear. This led me to believe I was a great disappointment to my father.

Another way my father thought he could cure me of my bed-wetting was to restrict my fluid intake, and he strictly enforced that no fluids would be drunk throughout the day without his permission. Moreover, my father gave me dry toast for breakfast, increasing my need for water.

Other times, he would have me go to bed immediately after supper. It was always the rule that I had to lie extremely still on my stomach, facing the wall; I could not curl up.

Once in bed, we were taught not to talk or move around; talking or moving around was a capital offense. My father would check in on us every few minutes. If we moved an inch, he would somehow know. I never understood how he knew, but he always did.

In a dysfunctional way, my favorite consequence for bed-wetting was being spanked. I say this because I favored temporary pain over wearing my wet undies all day. Looking back, I believe most of my bed-wetting problems were because I was stressed about making my dad happy. No matter how hard I tried to keep myself and the bed dry, I could not. I remember the immense anxiety over staying dry at night to please my father. The more I focused on fixing the problem, the worse it became.

Many times I would get up in the middle of the night, use the bathroom, and then get back into bed, only to wake up urine-soaked. I did not understand why I still wet the bed even though I had used the bathroom.

Bathing in our household was a bimonthly routine, primarily due to the cost of water. My parents told us they could not afford for us to wash daily, and this left me smelling of urine for weeks on end.

Anxiety and Food

Another source of my father's anger was my eating disorder. I tended to eat slowly, especially when eating meats or sandwiches. Since I was so limited on fluids, swallowing would often be extremely difficult. Once again, the situation appeared to intensify when I tried to please my father but could not.

We were taught to eat one food at a time, always beginning with the meat, which seemed to be the most difficult for me to swallow. I was forbidden to take a bite of something else on my plate that would make it easier for me. The more my father became upset, the worse my problem became.

I had to eat fast or else. Often, there was a timer set for me. If I did not finish before the timer went off, I had to go to bed without having anything else to eat or drink.

At times, my father would use my brother as the timer, which I did not particularly appreciate since he was a typical boy with no digestive issues and ate extremely fast. I could not keep up with him. As a result, mealtimes for me were filled with extreme stress and anxiety.

As children, we quickly learned never to tell our father what we did or did not like on our plates. The rule was that we always had to eat one thing at a time, beginning with the meat, and we had to eat everything on our plates. If it were known to him that we did not like something, we were given more of that item and made to eat it without any complaints.

I grew to hate sardines with a passion and still do to this day. When my father learned of my dispassion, he would pile more on my plate. I soon figured out how to use reverse psychology on my father and did not react when I had to eat them. Surprisingly, it worked. He eventually stopped giving me those disgusting, smelly little creatures to eat.

SCHOOL

Since my brother was the first male in the family, I always felt he had my father's approval without even trying. As time passed, I discovered I could earn my father's approval and acceptance by getting better grades than he did. He struggled in school, and I deliberately took advantage of it, knowing it was not right. I now viewed myself above him.

I worked hard to receive mostly As and Bs in school. Even though schoolwork was challenging, I could maintain my grades and learned that if I applied myself, I could succeed. Finally, this was one area of my life I could control.

In school, my brother was one grade ahead of me, but by the time I was in second grade, my brother had to repeat a year, making us in the same grade. Our school divided the students alphabetically. We were always in the same classroom, with me sitting before him since my name came first alphabetically. Often, staff and students perceived us to be twins even though there was a year between us.

Because we were in the same classroom, we became very close and would play together at recess. I remember he would defend me when someone picked on me, and I appreciated his protection.

Although I liked school, there were times when my body odor was so intense I was embarrassed. With no choice of remedy, I had to downplay it. I wore the same ugly, threadbare hand-me-downs the entire week and was taunted and teased constantly by many of my classmates because of my appearance. I was the kid with "cooties," and consequently, no one wanted to be my friend or sit near me.

Such cruel ostracism made me timid, and I did not make friends easily.

Though school was a painful experience, I dreaded the end of the day when I would have to return home. At least at school, I could move around, use the bathroom, and get a drink from the water fountain.

Since I came to school with body odor, bruises, and often little lunch to eat, one would think someone would have taken notice and said something. Not even the janitor noticed my pathetic state and its nonverbal communication of "Does anyone notice me?" or "Am I the only one with cooties?"

Much of my abuse occurred before mandated reporting became law. I was this tiny, thin, smelly kid who often came to school with a sandwich and just enough money for one little carton of milk. A couple of times, a teacher would feel sorry for me and buy a cupcake to accompany my sandwich, but no one would question my poor appearance.

I always believed our elderly neighbor lady, who often watched our property, knew of the abuse in our home. We lived close enough that she could hear the loud screaming, hollering, and breaking of household items, and she was close enough to witness how we were forced to behave. Why she never said anything, I do not know.

Not a word was spoken, at least to my knowledge, because people were taught to mind their own business, which was unfortunate for us. As children, we lived our lives behind our smiles. As I think about it, I am unsure if I would have said anything for fear of what would happen. After all, we lived by the rule of keeping secrets, and secrecy kept my father from getting into trouble. When summer vacation came around, I dreaded the three-month break because I would not have the modicum of peace or freedom I had at school.

APPROVAL SEEKING

To win my father's acceptance and approval, I did everything I could to comply with his rules and commands. I learned that my father enjoyed back massages, and I was the only one he would allow to do this, which made me feel extraordinarily important. When he became angry, I was obligated to massage his back. I felt strangely validated and wanted.

I discovered that if I snitched on my siblings when rules were broken, I earned my father's approval. I am not proud of this, but I was desperate for his acceptance. Besides, no one in the family had the bed-wetting problem as I did, which made me the constant object of his wrath.

In some distorted way, I held on to a delusional belief that I was still my father's favorite, though it came at a painful price. Whether the attention was positive or negative, it did not matter—at least it was attention.

If I were in trouble for something, my father would walk by and ignore me. Sometimes he would pinch my cheek and cause painful sores inside my mouth. Other times, he resorted to a violent face slap. If I objected or showed any signs of discomfort or tears, he would repeatedly do it.

This experience taught me to bury my emotions of anger and pain. I developed a distorted belief that my father did this because he liked me. This set the stage for me to allow others to mistreat me. Abuse became love—what a distortion!

At times, my father would grab the back of my neck and shake my head until I was dizzy. He thought it was funny and groomed me to believe the same. I thought this was a sign of endearment.

I received mixed messages when I thought that snitching on my siblings would somehow win my father's favor. The awful result was witnessing them pay the consequences.

UNDER THE INFLUENCE

Many nights my father would take me to the bars. This excited me and made me feel special. When we arrived at the bar, I was told to sit still and be quiet. Sometimes he introduced me to his drinking buddies. I enjoyed the frequent attention from his bar friends because they told me I was cute.

Other times, I was not allowed to go inside the bars with him; instead, I was forced to wait in the car. Whether I waited fifteen minutes or fifteen hours, I believed I had a special place in his heart. Looking back, I am amazed that he did not get me or one of my siblings killed.

My father had no fear of driving drunk, and there were so many close calls. He often drove over a hundred miles an hour just for fun. Other times, he taunted the driver in front of him by tailgating. In silence, I feared for my life. He would get so upset at the car in front of him that he would follow them for miles, hoping to scare them. Occasionally, he would get stopped by the police, but he was good at talking himself out of a ticket. I am not sure how he did this with alcohol on his breath, but he would always drive away with only a warning from the officer.

PUNISHMENTS, HURTS, AND DISAPPOINTMENTS

I had to go to bed early when I was not invited to the bars with my father. During these times, my siblings and I would talk about what life would be like as adults. Knowing our father would disapprove, we had to talk quietly so our mother would not hear us. These were times when we built a special bond.

Whenever I watched television, I prayed my father would not come home before I went to bed. If he did come home before I went to bed, I feared he would get angry with me for either how I was sitting or how I looked at him. I lived in terror of being punished for no reason. I learned the phrase "Out of sight, out of mind." I tried to become invisible, and this tactic seemed to work unless I was already in trouble for something else.

I lived in fear of going to sleep at night, wondering if my father would come in and terrorize me. He would frequently burst into the room, yelling and screaming for reasons I did not understand. This only increased my overwhelming anxiety.

Whenever my parents fought, it created knots in my stomach. Sometimes I would break my father's rule and not lie still in bed. I would press my ear against the wall and listen to what was happening on the other side. I remember praying to God that my father would not come into my bedroom. If he were frustrated or angry at my siblings for misbehaving that day, he would punish me for their misbehavior.

Our father would often pull our hair or throw us around like rag dolls. Sometimes my mother would attempt to intervene, but she risked having her own hair pulled or being tossed about the room, which made it worse for all of us. Often, we noticed the many bruises and bald spots our mother had. Any attempt on her part to help us was never a guarantee that we would be safe.

Sometimes our father thought he would have a little fun by having us wrestle with each other. He would make us put on boxing gloves and fight each other. My father often ordered me to strike my brother hard, causing him pain. I knew if I did not comply, I would be punished.

One night, my sister was the target of my father's drunkenness. She had broken his rules, so he threw her so hard that she nearly lost consciousness. I remember my mother called the police. Seeing my sister in such a state was scary for all of us.

When the police arrived, my mother recanted and said that she had called them by mistake. I was furious with her. How dare she protect our father and not our sister? Looking back, I realize she was terrified of her husband and made the decision for her own self-preservation.

EXTENDED ABUSIVE BEHAVIOR

My sister received the harshest abuse of all of us. I sensed my father never really liked her because she was strong-willed and often went against his grain. She often challenged him by disobeying his rules. Of course, this made him very angry. In retaliation, he would tie her ankles to the foot of her bed. He believed this would teach her a lesson and keep her in place.

Occasionally, my sister would be tied to a chair in the utility room. To ensure she did not move, our father propped matchsticks against the chair legs, thinking that if she tried to move, the matchsticks would fall to the floor. He would also sprinkle talcum powder around the chair to see her footprints if she got loose. I remember my father boastfully telling me how clever he was when disciplining my sister.

Every now and then, my father would find feces behind the washing machine. How it got there remained a mystery, but my best guess was that because we always had to have permission to use the bathroom, my sister had no choice but to do this or soil her underwear.

My father always told me and my siblings how stupid and ugly we were, adding that we were the most hideous children anyone could find. We had faces that could "stop a clock," and we would never amount to anything. If we showed any emotional reaction, we would be disciplined. We all developed low self-esteem as a result.

Let the Good Times Roll

When I was eight, my father allowed my older brother and me to attend vacation Bible school (VBS) at a small church down the road from us. The new young pastor came to our house one afternoon, asking my father if we could attend church during VBS week. After an hour of discussion, my father agreed. His response surprised me because he was so much against the church and intensely despised all preachers, especially if they were shoving scripture down his throat.

Fortunately, this young pastor did not attempt to do any of that. Instead, he tried to build a personal relationship with my father by playing one-on-one basketball in our driveway. No pastor had ever approached my father in this way.

After VBS was over, my father allowed my brother and me to attend church for a few Sundays. The church became one of my favorite places. There, everyone treated me as someone special.

It was not long before the young pastor left the church, and my father then prohibited us from attending anymore. This was the first time I was introduced to the Bible and its teachings. This ignited a spark deep within me and would one day change my life.

CHAPTER 2

The Preteen/Teen Years

Family is supposed to be a haven. Very often, it's
the place where we find the deepest heartache.

—Iyanla Vanzant

My preteen years were no different from my earlier years. They were
full of the same physical and emotional abuse. When I was eleven,
my mother told me and my siblings about several knife incidents
between her and our father. A couple of times, when he came home
intoxicated, he had become angry and thrown a knife at her, thank-
fully being too drunk to hit his target.

I remember hearing my mother's bloodcurdling screams
through the thin bedroom walls of our home. In the morning, when
we woke up, we discovered holes in the walls where our father had
punched his fists the night before. We would also find broken furniture or other items my mother treasured. The holes would remain in
the walls for many years as a reminder of what would occur if anyone
made him angry.

When I was twelve, our lives were drastically changed when
our father obtained a job as a mechanic at a local gas station down
the street. He enjoyed his job and worked four days a week. With
his renewed sense of purpose and value, his abusive behaviors and
drinking subsided somewhat.

FAMILY AND ADDICTIONS

My father's income did not go toward paying any household bills; instead, it went toward alcohol and cigarettes. This upset my mother, but at least her income went toward the household and not toward her husband's addictions. This helped relieve some of the tension in our home.

Sometimes, on my father's days off, he would allow my older brother and me to stay home from school. He would take us fishing or drive us to a nearby town to explore the sites. These were memorable times with him that I enjoyed.

Around this time, our paternal grandfather moved from Florida to Indiana, which had a positive influence on my father. I enjoyed having my grandfather around; he always laughed and told funny stories. I later learned that my grandfather had alcohol and nicotine addictions like my father. Unlike my father, however, my grandfather had broken free from his addictions earlier in his adult life.

My grandfather suffered severe heart attacks and lung cancer when he was younger. He told me his heart attacks convinced him to quit drinking and smoking. Sadly, he had one of his lungs removed due to cancer.

I always admired that my grandfather could quit both addictions with minimal effort once he decided to stop. I wished my father would have that same desire, and I was instilled with some hope that he would also overcome his addictions.

Fond memories of my grandfather included fishing, camping, and playing cards. My grandfather was proud of how much money he had saved by quitting drinking and smoking. He also told me he was saddened by how his son had picked up his addictions and that he saw the devastation it had caused to our family.

One day, after an explosive argument with my mother, my father took me to the bar. After a few drinks, he became strangely transparent. He shared his regrets about how he had treated us, saying that he couldn't help himself. His words completely minimized ownership of his abuse. This left me feeling distraught.

He continued to justify his strictness, saying that he was easily agitated. He further shared his struggles with being a healthy parent. I learned a great deal about his unhappiness with life and with himself. Though his confessions touched me deeply, I was left with conflicted emotions of feeling honored and empathetic, yet sad and angry toward him.

Upon returning home, my father became upset with me for some unknown reason. Realizing my father had too much to drink, I was concerned about what he might do to me. My instincts were correct as he beat me mercilessly.

The anger on his face turned to rage as he threw me around the room. After a few minutes of being tossed around, I felt a sharp pain in my foot. When my father ceased his violence, he told me to sit in the utility room where my sister was sent for punishment. I can still feel the pain in my foot today, though being sent to the laundry room and isolated was more painful at the time.

In my humiliation, I cried out to God, pleading for the beatings to stop. Even though I did not know God as my personal Savior, I prayed, "God, if you are real, please stop my father from being so angry at me and hurting me. I cannot take the shame and the pain anymore."

Amazingly, within a few minutes, my father came into the utility room with a different attitude, telling me that I could go out and play. I have goosebumps as I write this.

Answered Prayer

God answered my prayer. He revealed to me that he was real, caring, and loving in a personal way I had never experienced. Without a doubt, I knew that he had heard my prayer and my plea for help.

My encounter with God inspired me to know him more personally. I remember thinking that I needed to learn more about this loving, caring God, not the one my father had described. I wanted a love that would care for me and protect me.

Spiritual Journey

Spiritually, I was different from most local teens my age since religion was not an essential foundation in our family. We did not pray or value having God at the center of our lives like many families in the Bible Belt.

Neither of my siblings showed any interest in exploring their spirituality, and I am sure this contributed to my sense of disconnection. All I knew was that I did not want to live like my family did, especially like my father.

I knew something was missing when it came to watching *Billy Graham Crusades* on television and hearing the Word of God, which ignited something inside me. My father knew I wanted to watch Billy Graham, so he occasionally sat down with me, and we watched it together. I never understood how he could not be affected by hearing God's Word. Regardless, just having my father take the time to sit with me filled my heart with joy.

As we watched the *Crusades* together, my father constantly reminded me that religion was not a thing for him. Often, he would blurt out "You know, a person needs to clean up first" or "God will throw you out of the church, ya know, if you are a bad person." Although I tried to tell him otherwise, he would not listen. My father's god was alcohol and cigarettes, leaving no room for the true God I was beginning to know.

As a result of attending VBS, I had my own Bible, which I hid under my bed for fear of getting into trouble for reading it. I would wake up when the sun rose to have enough light to read by. I knew my father would disapprove of my time spent reading the Bible, let alone waking up early. My thirst for learning about God was now my focus, and I wanted to know more about his love for me.

I enjoyed sitting on our twin-seat porch swing and reading one of my favorite books on quiet afternoons. I knew my father would disapprove, so I would read when he was at work. Some of my favorite books were the Bobbsey Twins series and anything to do with animals or nursing. I wanted to be a nurse when I grew up. I also wanted a life filled with joy, peace, and God.

One day I had an aha moment with my father and his drinking friends at the bar. I experienced clarity as to what sort of life I wanted. I knew I never wanted to marry someone like my father, and I wanted God to be the center of my life. Ironically, my father turned toward me, not knowing my thoughts, and said, "Life is like a deck of cards. You play with what you are dealt. A person cannot change—life does not change."

A MOMENT OF FREEDOM

I had to go to the hospital for three days for testing due to having circulatory problems in my legs. Although I was scared at first, I found the brief stay enjoyable as I was away from the family chaos. What I enjoyed most was choosing what I ate and drank. This was never an option at home. I could also decide what I wanted to watch on television, and I had the freedom to call my friends on the phone. This experience helped open my eyes to a life of choices.

The night I came home from the hospital, my father asked if I wanted to play some cards. Of course, I said yes. What made this different was that my father did not smell like beer like he did after a heavy night of drinking. Being that there was no smell, I assumed I was safe.

Because I was more focused on playing cards with my father, I did not keep count of the many beers he drank. He began yelling and screaming at me as we played, telling me I was acting "cocky." He accused me of thinking I was special just because I had been in the hospital. He said that I was "worthless."

When my mother came in from the living room to see what was happening, I shouted impulsively, "Old Lady, you don't need to protect me!" My *father* interpreted this as me calling out for help. He hurled his half-full beer bottle at me, barely missing my face. The bottle hit the wall and broke into little pieces. I was then told the beer stains on the wall were my fault. The stains remained on the wall for many years. Whenever my father walked past that beer-stained wall, I would hear him shout how awful I was.

My father created what was known as "fun nights." Fun nights included coming home from a night of drinking and wanting to horse around with us. On one occasion, something went terribly wrong.

My father had me stand on my brother's top bunk, with him grabbing my ankles; he then flipped me in the air, which landed me on my sister's bed, about six feet away. My head hit the edge of the window frame, causing a deep wound about an inch long under my left eye. As you would imagine, blood came spurting out. I was crying and screaming in excruciating pain.

My mother heard my screams and came running into the bedroom. She saw my bloody face and immediately screamed at my father. He remained reticent, which was highly unusual for him. I believe the shock of seeing the bloody gash under my eye was a sobering moment for him. My mother quickly bandaged my wound and wrapped it with tape to stop the bleeding.

Two days after the incident, my father became less controlling of me and gave me more freedom. Although I was still in pain from my injury, I appreciated the freedom and space I now had.

Returning to school after several days off, my seventh-grade teacher looked at my black eye and my bruised face and asked me what had happened. I told her I accidentally fell out of bed. I had been groomed by my father to protect him from any harm. The teacher accepted my story.

MISCHIEVOUS SISTER

During my teen years, my sister had severe problems due to receiving what I believe to be the harshest emotional and physical abuse of us all.

My parents received calls from a teacher who stated that items were missing from her classroom. They were told that the items would most likely be found in my sister's desk or locker. Strangely enough, there were also items missing from our home. As it turned out, the missing items from school and the missing items from home were found in my sister's locker.

The concerned principal strongly encouraged my sister to get professional help by seeing a psychiatrist. My parents arranged for treatment, but after a few visits, my father decided that she was receiving too much positive attention and discontinued her sessions.

Not long afterward, I was home alone with my sister on one of those rare times when my father would allow us to go outside together and play. While we were playing, a white station wagon pulled into our driveway. I became concerned as I did not recognize the car. I looked around for my sister and did not see her. Feeling scared, I called out to her. Suddenly, I heard a car door slam and turned to see the station wagon back down the driveway and drive off. As it turned out, my sister had arranged for her friend's parents to pick her up so she could run away.

When my parents came home and asked where my sister was, I told them about the station wagon. My father was furious with me for not watching over her more carefully. Instead of calling the police, my parents searched for her everywhere but could not find her.

A few days later, I visited my grandmother, who lived a few miles down the road. I discovered some of my sister's clothes tucked under a bed in the upstairs bedroom. Suddenly, it hit me: my sister had run away to live with our grandmother.

Knowing the truth about my sister, I feared keeping her secret safe. I became anxious, wondering what I would say if my mother or father asked me. When they eventually did ask me, I blurted out, "She's over at Grandma's!"

After my sister ran away, my father would claim that he only had three children and not four. I felt sad for my sister, and it was not until our father's passing years later that she reconnected with the family.

MY BROTHER'S CHALLENGE

My older brother began getting into legal trouble because of drug and alcohol use. When he got a car, he was not prepared for the new freedoms he would have. His vehicle would often have broken windows and dents due to his reckless driving habits.

Drugs and alcohol began to take control of his life. With no guidance or support, he was on a downward spiral. Consequently, he dropped out of school with only one semester left in his senior year. I felt sad because we did not graduate together as I thought we would.

Shortly after dropping out of school, he met a lady at a bar and married her. The marriage did not last as they divorced within the year due to his continued drug and alcohol use.

The Birds and the Bees

My mother and father never discussed the "birds and the bees" with me. The first mention of anything to do with sex was when I was ten years old. Out of the blue, my father told me that someday I would lie naked with a man. Feeling grossed out, I did not want to talk anymore about sex. I remember telling my father I would never be naked with a man. Of course, he laughed at me, leaving me even angrier, although I did not show it for fear of being hit. Out of frustration, I attempted to convince him that I would never touch a man that way or have him feel me that way. Of course, he continued laughing.

To make matters worse, my father asked my mother if she thought I would lie naked with a man. To my surprise, she said yes, and I was devastated. Soon after, my father began to show me pictures from magazines of people having sex. It was all so disturbing.

Around this time, I noticed public displays of affection between my mother and father. My father often groped my mother's breasts, and her responses told me that public displays of affection were inappropriate.

When I was twelve, my parents handed me a set of books. These books were not the type I would typically read. The books were about helping me understand how my body would change, especially during a girl's teen years. This was not the kind of reading I enjoyed, but I read it because my father told me to. I do not remember learning about healthy sexuality or intimacy. Instead, I learned the mechanics of the male and female sex organs.

During my health and safety classes in school, I learned more about my body and about sex. Around this time, my father reminded me that I would one day sleep naked with a man. I remember feeling disgusted by the idea and became annoyed with him for even mentioning this to me.

I am sure my negative view of sex resulted from my father showing me pictures from his pornography collections. Not only did my father routinely show me his collection but he also showed me what he referred to as his "special toys." He told me it was essential to have sex toys and why he liked them.

High School

High school for me was a more positive experience than elementary and middle school. I was not teased as much and could make a few new friends. Also, my grades and personal view of myself improved.

There was only one exception, and that was gym class. Because I was uncoordinated, I did not do well in sports. I dreaded when the teacher picked the team captain and had them take turns choosing their team members. I would always be the last one picked and was subjected to sarcastic comments.

During a game, I was approached by one of my team members who scolded me for not getting the ball over the net. She went on to say she would beat me up if I did not hit the ball over the net.

As a result, I experienced a high level of fear and anxiety. The following day, I tried my best to get out of gym class. No excuses I made worked, so I devised plan B. I would inform the teacher that I was being bullied. Something told me not to go through with it, for fear I would pay a price for tattling. Ironically, the teammate who threatened to beat me up became my friend in my senior year.

Sophomore Year

One of the most fearful times during my sophomore year was when I was called to the school's administrative office. I remember experiencing terrible stomach cramps, much like I would have when my period started. I felt a tremendous heaviness as I walked to the office as I had never been summoned prior. For sure I was in trouble, or my father, for some reason, had created a problem for me.

When I arrived, I was informed that I was the only student from a low-income family chosen by the school to work in the front office. This was part of a new government program designed to help low-income families earn more money. The program allowed me to work up to ten hours weekly at minimum wage.

Though I was seen as coming from a low-income family, I did not care. I felt unique and important because I was recognized for being *someone*. I felt honored and special—a rarity in my life.

When I came home from school that day, I asked my dad if I could work in the front office. Usually, I would have hesitated to ask, but this time, for some reason, I felt safe. Without hesitation, my father said yes.

During the following summer, I had the opportunity to work about twenty-five hours per week, which helped me earn some money. I valued saving money from my weekly paychecks so I could one day live independently outside my parents' home.

I experienced two other benefits from this special program. One was that my self-esteem dramatically increased, and the other was that I was able to purchase contact lenses. I have worn glasses since the fifth grade.

I saved enough money to purchase a moped. This provided quick and easy transportation to and from school. Having a taste of financial freedom offered me choices I never had before. This, too, increased my positive self-esteem.

I began to think about my future education. Knowing my parents would not contribute toward college, I started to put money away.

When I was a junior in high school, I was stalked by a male student. After finishing my work for the day in the office, this student managed to pin me against a locker and grope my breasts. Terrified, I quickly pushed him away and ran as fast as I could down the hallway without looking back.

When I arrived home, I immediately told my father, believing he would do something to protect me and stop the boy from ever doing it again. To my disappointment, my father became furious and told me it was *always* the female's fault. He said that if a girl were raped, then she must have done something to deserve it.

My father claimed that I must have enticed this boy to touch me and that it was not his fault. I began to cry and tried to tell him that I had done nothing wrong, but he only became more enraged, telling me to "shut the hell up!"

I felt alone and angry that my father blamed me for what had happened. I wanted to run to my bedroom and slam the door as hard as I could, but I knew if I did, I would get beaten. With a heavy heart, I suppressed my feelings and pushed them deep down inside me.

In my confusion, I began to consider my father's words. Maybe it was my fault? I must have done something to provoke this boy. My thinking patterns continued to be distorted.

Driver's Education

Of course, most teenagers cannot wait to get their driver's license, and I was no different. I took driver's education at school when I was sixteen as it was part of the school's academic program.

Most kids in the class had prior driving experience as their parents often took them out to practice, whereas my parents did not. My father did not take me out to practice because he had a manual shift and knew I would be driving an automatic. I could not practice at home and felt very inadequate and stupid.

When it was my turn to sit in the driver's seat, I was nervous and self-conscious. I might have caused several students in the back seat to wet themselves due to my driving over curbs when making right-hand turns. Regardless of how often I tried to exercise my classroom learnings, I would run up and down curbs with too many unnecessary, sudden stops.

Regarding parallel parking, I took the prize for hitting the most curbs. It became clear that driving would not come easy for me. The students who drove the best with the instructor received a waiver from having to take the driving test at the licensing bureau. Of course, I was not one of those lucky students.

Eventually, when I finished my senior year of high school, I retook driver's ed during the summer. Surprisingly, my driving had improved. I was the only person in the class who received a waiver. I remember telling myself, "God is good."

After graduating high school, I felt good about myself, especially since I graduated in the top 10 percent of my class. I was looking forward to moving away to college to study nursing in the fall. For the first time in my life, I would have complete freedom, or so I thought.

CHAPTER 3

The Early Adult Years

Sometimes the bad things that happen in
our lives put us directly on the path to the
best things that will ever happen to us.

—Unknown

Before I begin to recount my journey into young adulthood, I need
to revisit my junior year of high school. That year, I had two friends
to whom I was particularly drawn because they wanted to discuss
God. I had a burning desire to learn more about God, especially after
watching a few *Billy Graham Crusades* on television.

Both girls were interested in starting a Bible study during our
lunch period. However, they were from two different walks of faith:
one was a Jehovah's Witness, and the other was a Southern Baptist.
Not knowing the difference, I was not concerned and thought anything I could learn would be beneficial.

The Jehovah's Witness had a bubbly personality and was
extremely friendly and gracious to everyone. In contrast, the Southern
Baptist was quieter and more reserved. For some odd reason, both
competed for my attention. I was more drawn to the bubbly personality of the Jehovah's Witness.

I enjoyed being in a Bible study with my new friends. One evening, I came home excited and shared this with my father. Thinking
he would be proud of me, he instead became outraged. He told

me without hesitation that if I became friends with any Jehovah's Witness, I had to pack all my belongings and leave *his* home. I was confused and did not know where his anger was coming from. Why was he referring to my home as *his* home?

Consequently, I ended my relationship with my Jehovah's Witness friend. The next day, I told her I could not be friends because we did not share the same spiritual beliefs. To this day, I regret ending my relationship with her based on my father's ultimatum.

Interestingly, my father did not prevent me from having a relationship with my Southern Baptist friend, so we continued studying together. We became close friends. She taught me how to pray and would occasionally ask me to close in prayer after our studies. I was flattered that she thought of me enough to pray with her.

I was still a junior in high school, and I knew I would not be allowed the freedom to attend church while living at home. If I were to seek a relationship with God, it would have to wait until I left home.

Adult Spiritual Growth

My journey began with the concept of either living eternally in heaven or eternally in hell. This made me look for a church where I could learn the truth about heaven and hell. I knew that sinners went to hell and repenting sinners went to heaven. I also knew that God was what I needed if I wanted to go to heaven.

Within the first two weeks of college, I found a church to attend. The same quiet, reserved Southern Baptist friend who led me in Bible study during my junior year ironically attended the same college. She invited me to attend her Wednesday evening prayer group. Of course, I said yes, but I developed a sinking feeling in my gut that she might also ask me to join her church, which I did not want to do.

After one night of study and prayer, she did exactly that; she asked if I wanted to meet with the church pastor. Feeling excited yet fearful, I consented.

The pastor was welcoming and friendly. After the initial pleasantries, he asked me if I knew that everyone is born a sinner. Before I could answer, he quoted Romans 3:10 (NIV), "As it is written: There is no one righteous, not even one." He proceeded to quote Romans 3:23 (NIV), "For all have sinned and fall short of the glory of God."

I did not have a problem recognizing that I was a sinner; my father often reminded me of how bad I was. The pastor then shared that God loved me so much, which seemed unbelievable to me because, once again, I was constantly reminded of how worthless I was as a child.

The pastor then read John 3:16 (NIV), "For God so loved the world that He gave His one and only Son, that whoever believes in Him shall not perish but have eternal life." This was difficult for me to comprehend. Why would God love someone like me so much that he would have his Son die for me? He asked me if I believed this, and I said yes because I did not know what else to say.

The pastor asked me if I knew how to receive God's forgiveness, and this time, I was honest and said no. So he read Romans 10:9–10 (NLT), which said, "If you openly declare that Jesus is Lord and believe in your heart that God raised him from the dead, you will be saved. For it is by believing in your heart that you are made right with God, and it is by openly declaring your faith that you are saved."

It did not take much time for the pastor to convince me what I needed to do. That night, I accepted the invitation to become a believer.

The pastor asked me to repeat after him, stating that I knew I was a sinner, that I believed that Jesus died for my wrongdoings, and that I wanted Jesus to come into my life and be Lord.

After accepting Jesus as my personal Lord and Savior, I thought something supernatural would happen. Yet I did not feel anything different other than the excitement others had for me for becoming "saved." Subsequently, I no longer feared death or dying, for I knew I would go to heaven.

Accepting Jesus Christ into my life also allowed me to start making my own decisions—decisions my father could not interfere with. By receiving Christ in my life, I could learn a new way of living that was much different than how I was raised.

Baptism

The pastor also advised that I should get baptized as soon as possible. With much support and encouragement, I agreed. However, I did not fully understand all this at the time.

Within two weeks, I was baptized at my friend's church. I was excited to see everyone else excited and happy for me. Soon after being baptized, the pastor discussed connecting me with a Bible-based student group at the college. Finally, someone wanted to invest in me. Everything was new and different. Still, I could hear my father's voice telling me he disapproved of these choices I was now making.

Joining the Bible study group helped quench my thirst for spiritual knowledge. I enjoyed studying the Bible and being active in the community with other believers. One of my fondest memories was going on hayrides. I had never experienced this agrarian tradition. We had so much fun throwing hay at one another and joking around. Also, we ended the night with s'mores and hot cocoa around a campfire. All this was such a new experience! That first night with the group was so amazing, and I had never felt so free and loved in my life.

It did not take long for me to accept this group of enthusiastic students as my family. Not long afterward, I was allowed to take a minor leadership role. Not only did that help me with my low self-esteem issues, it also helped me develop my leadership skills.

I cannot say enough about how this group helped me to feel unique and special. I finally had friends who loved and accepted me for simply being me.

SPIRITUAL BELIEFS

Being naive, I thought being a believer would exempt me from life's problems. I also thought that all believers were trustworthy people. Soon afterward, I learned a hard and valuable lesson.

Leaving home for college provided freedoms I never had before. Life would be picture-perfect and free of struggles as I did not have to answer to anyone or anything. I would no longer face emotional ridicule or physical and sexual abuse.

However, I still heard my father's disapproving voice echoing in my head whenever I made a decision. His haunting voice followed me throughout my young adulthood, creating confusion and chaos.

I began to struggle academically and quickly realized how difficult college was. It did not take long to discover I was unprepared.

On the first day of nursing class, we were asked to look at the person to our left and then to our right. The professor stated that one of us would not make it through the four years of training. I was horrified. Was she referring to me? Although I was determined not to be the one, I could hear my father's voice reminding me I was a failure.

Though I had earned As and Bs in high school, college was a struggle. It seemed the more I studied, the worse my grades became. Perhaps my father's voice and the professor's words might have heavily influenced my mind.

I was devastated when I flunked my first final in the fall. I studied for hours, which helped build my confidence; however, when it was time to take the final exam, my brain went blank, and I could not remember anything I had studied.

As a result, I received a D in my nursing class, having to retake the course the following year. I took this as confirmation of my father's words and the professor's warning: I was the one who would fail.

SOCIAL LIFE

My social skills were profoundly underdeveloped due to my father's rule of separating me and my siblings as children. Being socially challenged, it was hard to maintain relationships, and I was very self-conscious about what others thought of me. This made me a people pleaser because I deeply desired to be liked. After numerous exhausting attempts, I found my approach was not working.

I remember a college student named Barb who was in Bible study with me. She was very annoying and boisterous, constantly whining about anything and everything. This, of course, got under my skin. In thinking about addressing this, I privately discussed it with the group leader, asking if he felt the same, and if he did, could he say something to her?

He advised that I needed to learn how to get along with the Barbs of the world because there would always be people like Barb in my life.

Looking back, he was so right. Rather than trying to change others, I needed to change how I responded to difficult people.

BED-WETTING

Even during my college years, my bed-wetting remained a struggle. I felt extreme shame and embarrassment for not having outgrown this adolescent behavior. No matter how hard I tried, I was a big disappointment to myself.

I cannot imagine that my roommate was not aware. When I did not have time to do my laundry, I would make my bed to cover up the wet spot and spray it with room deodorizer, doing my best to hide my embarrassment. Consequently, laundry was a challenge. I would do my laundry when no one else was around so they did not have to smell my urine-soaked belongings. Whenever I threw my laundry in the washer, reeking of urine stench, it reminded me of my father's disgust. This only exacerbated my feelings of self-loathing, and the problem became worse.

When I would go on overnight outings, whether camping, traveling, or weekend retreats, I would have to make sure I got up early to check if I had wet the bed. If I did, I quickly removed the sheets and blankets and hid them for fear of others finding out about my issue. My bed-wetting fostered emotional and physical exhaustion.

Freedom of Choice

College life offered me the freedom of choice I never had growing up. I was excited to be free to choose what I ate and drank, whatever and whenever. I could now eat and drink without hearing the word *no* or secretly having to go behind my father's back.

Freedom also allowed me to join a Bible study group without fearing my father's censure. No longer did I worry about having to end friendships. No longer would I be held accountable to anyone other than myself.

Although I was used to living under strict rules and discipline, I was not applying any of these rules to my college life. Rather than prioritizing study time, I indulged in many midnight pizzas or ice cream binges with my friends. Although it felt good to have freedom, I was not setting healthy boundaries. This became painfully apparent when I went home, and my father would tell me that I was getting fat.

To this day, because of my father's criticism, I constantly worry about my body weight. I might have left home and the source of my low self-esteem, but I carried my negative self-image with me.

Financial Concerns

Finances became a struggle. My father had made it clear he would not provide any financial support, so I had to figure out how to support myself. I underestimated the financial responsibility of paying for school and living independently.

My first year was easy since I had a few scholarships and grants, but my grades quickly sank, and so did my financial assistance. All my financial support promptly vanished.

During the summer months after my sophomore year, when finances were worrisome, I worked as an aide at the local hospital. I would work as many hours as possible, saving every penny for my education, but it was still insufficient. Summer was a time of extra expenses, like rent, food, and household items. No matter how many hours I worked, I never really had enough.

A friend introduced me to selling cosmetics, and I soon discovered I did not have the personality or social skills to succeed. My other choice was to take on a part-time job, as my friends did, but that would take away from my needed study time. I did not know what to do. Once again, the echoing voice inside my head screamed that I was a failure and that my future was not promising.

TURN FOR THE WORSE

Struggling with my low self-esteem and toxic shame, I slid deeper into feelings of unworthiness. The intensity was so great that I started to question my college choice. The extreme emotional pain pierced the very fabric of my soul.

My mind raced with thoughts that I was unimportant and unworthy. Internal voices told me I should drop out of college, drop out of Bible study, and simply disappear. I was a failure at everything, and my only choice, it seemed, was to become invisible.

One day, the emotional agony became so severe that I took a handful of cold medicine pills. I did not want to die, but I did not want to feel the pain anymore.

My roommate discovered what I had done. She was both frightened and angry at the same time. After talking with her, I promised to never do it again. Through this experience, I learned that I did, in fact, matter. However, my father's voice crept back in, telling me otherwise.

GETTING BACK ON MY FEET AGAIN

I found solace by staying focused, attending college, attending church, and sticking with my Bible study groups. I loved learning from both the church and Bible study. I was hungry for God's Word and wanted to be around people who would accept me as I was.

I found a new church a few miles from where I lived. I befriended the pastor and his wife by sharing my story. They were a young couple who had only been married for a decade and had been in the ministry for only a few years. They had a heart for college students. I felt as though their hearts were filled with love and compassion. I loved attending this new church because I thought I was finally in a healthy family of believers.

One cold Friday night in February, I accepted an invitation to spend the weekend with my pastor and his family. It would be a welcome break from the pressures of living in the college dorm.

They had two beautiful twin boys who were active toddlers. After dinner, the boys were tucked away in bed for the night. The pastor's wife stated she was exhausted and going to bed. That left the pastor and me sitting on the couch, watching television.

Thinking nothing of the situation, I sat up with him and chatted. I felt safe. After all, he was a pastor. As the evening progressed, the pastor grabbed my hands and caressed them. An alarm went off inside me, but I reminded myself that he was my pastor and that I was supposed to trust him. Not having reference to what was normal or healthy, I allowed him to caress my hands even though I sensed something was wrong.

The pastor got more comfortable caressing my hands. To my horror, he took my hands and put them in his lap. Shocked and paralyzed, I was in an extreme state of confusion.

I noticed he had an erection. I quickly pulled my hand away, but he grabbed it back and placed it on his crotch. My mind spun, trying to decide what to do. Finally, I moved when he inserted his hand into the back of my blue jeans. I quickly got up and excused myself, stating I needed to go to bed.

The next day, neither the pastor nor I mentioned anything about the incident the night before. It wasn't until a few days later when he called me and told me to come to his office.

When I met with him at the church office, he profusely apologized for his actions and made me promise never to tell anyone. He said it was a one-time situation. I promised I would say nothing and left his office, feeling unsettled and confused. My father's voice told me it was all my fault. I recalled his words, "It is always the woman's fault if a man violates her." I experienced even more toxic shame and self-loathing. I had thought men of faith were the only men to be trusted, and I was left with only one conclusion: it *was* my fault.

I never shared the secret of my pastor's predatorial interaction with me. It would be a secret I kept deep inside for years to come.

MISSION TRIP

I enjoyed being part of the campus Bible study group and attended every weekly meeting. I shared *some* of my struggles, both spoken and unspoken. I felt connected to the group because they were college peers who could relate to the various stresses of college life.

During the summer after my freshman year, my group planned a ten-week mission trip to four areas, including Chicago, Illinois; Nipawin, Saskatchewan, Canada; North Pole, Alaska; and Glorieta, New Mexico.

Our mission activities included creating and performing skits, singing, and sharing our testimonies. I especially looked forward to creating and performing the skits because they helped me feel valued and appreciated.

I was fortunate to have the entire summer available for the mission trip and raised enough money. It would be an experience I knew I would never forget.

It was an inspiring ten weeks. About a dozen college students participated, with three adult leaders guiding us. We took two vehicles, one towing a trailer with our ministry and camping supplies and the other filled with laughter, joy, and excitement. Our plans included sleeping in tents at various churches while on the road.

While in a small community near Wisconsin, we went door-to-door seeking interested people desiring to start a new church plant. We fell in love with the community and our connection with the pastor and his wife. For the most part, we all got along and worked well as a team.

Going door-to-door was out of my comfort zone; fear of who or what was behind the door made me feel extremely vulnerable. When the door opened, we would ask if they had a church home, and if they did not, we would invite them to attend a new church plant.

We would canvass the neighborhood in pairs to provide safety if something were to happen. For the most part, we experienced a good response. Because of my social awkwardness, I would stand back and allow my partner to do most of the talking.

We spent a week ministering in this small community. I also had the opportunity to tour the city of Chicago. Since I was studying nursing, I was in awe of the vastness of the hospitals and the buildings connected to them.

I was impressed with our first stop and having the opportunity to work with this young pastor and his wife. Starting a church plant was exciting, along with seeing such large hospitals. I remember thinking I would return as a nurse one day, working at one of the local hospitals and becoming a new church member.

After a week in Illinois, we packed the vehicles and journeyed for ten days to Nipawin, Saskatchewan, Canada. The drive proved to be a magnificent view of the country, and we did the same in Nipawin, Saskatchewan, as in Chicago, Illinois.

In the mornings, we would canvass the neighborhoods, seeking interest in forming a new church plant. In the afternoons, we would hold children's Bible studies in the pastor's yard.

We enjoyed getting to know the people and their culture, and it was exciting because it was much different than what I was used to.

After a week in Canada, we packed up and traveled the Alaskan Highway to North Pole, Alaska. I thought this would be a straightforward journey, but it was far from it.

Before starting out again, we were told we needed to ensure our vehicle's radiators were covered with a wire mesh screen. This was partly due to the dirt roads being covered with loose gravel. Because of the loose gravel, stones would get kicked up from the cars traveling ahead of us and cause radiator punctures.

Because gas stations, restaurants, and roadside bathrooms were rare, we had to plan strategically. The most difficult challenge was when it came to bathroom breaks. We stopped about every hour or so to stretch and pee. The women were instructed to take some toilet paper and go to the side of the road, where they would go without being seen. The men, of course, were instructed to go to the other side of the road, line up with their backsides to the cars, and pee. This became our norm for many days on the road.

Toward the end of each day of travel, we would pull off on the side of the road and find a safe area to set up our camp. We were reminded to be alert because wild animals were in the area. With eyes wide open for what seemed like the entire night, I tried to get some sleep.

We were forced to camp in one area for a few nights because the road had been washed away by a torrential rainfall. The "highway people," as we called them, had to plow out a new route for us. We had a very adventurous time during this part of the trip.

Arriving just outside of North Pole, Alaska, part of our schedule was to stop and paint a local church. It was a welcome change from knocking on doors.

Some of our adventures included panning for gold, sightseeing on Mount McKinley, and eating barbecue moose. We also enjoyed getting to know one another.

Another unique experience was having daylight for twenty-three hours, while the remaining hour was like dusk, never becoming completely dark. Surprisingly, adapting to sleeping in the bright sunlight did not take long.

After a week in North Pole, Alaska, we packed up and headed south to the Glorieta Retreat Center in Glorieta, New Mexico.

Every summer, college students from all over the country would come to the retreat center to hear spiritual messages and worship together. While enjoying our time there, the retreat center heard about our ten-week mission trip and asked if we would share our experiences. Of course, we said yes, but we did not realize it would be in front of thousands.

This ten-week mission trip was a life-changing experience that created many great memories for me. Although I had some inner personal challenges, I learned to suppress them and lock them away.

My continued bed-wetting caused me the greatest concern. Many mornings I would wake up early, only to realize I had wet my sleeping bag. I did my best to air out my sleeping bag, trying to keep it hidden from others as there were no opportunities to wash it. I cannot imagine others were not wondering why I was constantly airing out my sleeping bag.

FRESHMAN YEAR DO-OVER

College life continued to be a challenge. I struggled with my grades, finances, and social skills. I was becoming increasingly aware of how unprepared I was.

Almost every negative college experience I had reminded me of how I was such a failure. My college friends were moving on while I had to repeat my freshman-year nursing classes. The same familiar voice told me I was unworthy and destined to remain a failure.

All my friends from my Bible study group were moving on too. I felt very isolated and alone. Life appeared dismal and dark as I struggled through the next two and a half years.

One of the few resources I had to help me through this struggle was during my mission trip to Chicago, Illinois, where I met a pastor and his family. I called them frequently to share my frustrations regarding my class challenges and social deficiencies. Understanding my concerns, they encouraged me to transfer my credits to a local college near them.

Within a day or two, I sought approval for a credit transfer. To my surprise, I received a letter of acceptance a week later. This motivated me to refocus and begin my new college experience.

My living conditions were also addressed when the pastor and his wife offered me a room at their country home if I agreed to help babysit their two adorable little girls. Without hesitation, I said yes as it seemed to answer my prayers. It did not take me long to pack up my belongings, buy a bus ticket, and relocate to Chicago. It took all the money I had saved to make the trip, but it was worth it.

While on the bus, I envisioned what my new life would be like. After all, I would have a fresh start living with a Christian family in a small town outside of Chicago. What could ever go wrong?

It did not take long for things to line up as planned—well, almost as planned. I loved living with the pastor, his wife, and their two young daughters, ages four and seven. The girls were full of energy and helped me feel very much loved, which I desperately hungered for.

They lived in the country where wheat fields and cornfields could be seen for miles. I enjoyed taking long walks on the country roads and breathing in the fresh country air. There were many days where huge cumulus clouds floated lazily across blue skies. In time, I found a nursing assistant job connected with the local clinic.

Only a few of my college credits had been transferred, so I would have to start over. Although disappointed at first, I did not let it get me down. I was bound and determined to get an education. If starting over was what I had to do, so be it. I went to school part-time and worked full-time to pay for my education.

By this time, I was learning to roll with the punches. After all, I had a purpose and lived with a truly Christian family. After I became a Christian, one of my dreams was to be a part of a Christian family. I felt like nothing could go awry; I was living the dream.

I truly enjoyed working at the hospital and meeting many interesting people as I floated from unit to unit. One time, I met a Saudi Arabian princess and her bodyguards. I suddenly appreciated my personal freedom.

Another time, I met my idol, Billy Graham. I told myself that if I ever met Billy Graham, I would ask him questions about heaven and God.

During one of my evening shifts, I was fortunate enough to be assigned to the same unit his wife was in. While delivering her dinner tray, I noticed the curtains around her bed were shut. To my surprise, the curtains opened, and Billy Graham was there facing me. He reached for the tray and said, "Thank you." I responded "Hi" and handed him the tray. I left feeling starstruck.

Life was good. I worked full-time, attended college part-time, and lived rent-free in exchange for babysitting. Going to college part-time helped me create better study habits, resulting in better grades. In my spare time, I enjoyed leisurely walks, reading books, and listening to Christian music. I enjoyed this new rhythm to my life.

Working at the hospital, I thoroughly enjoyed learning and caring for patients. I especially enjoyed hearing their stories and the struggles they shared. It quickly reminded me that I was not alone.

One of my responsibilities at the hospital was giving patients back massages. My patients often thanked me by telling me how they appreciated it; hearing this day after day helped boost my self-esteem.

I also gave the pastor and his wife shoulder massages using my newfound talent. They, too, thanked me by telling me how good it felt. Little did I know it would lead to trouble.

HISTORY REPEATING ITSELF

During that summer, the pastor's wife asked me if I could take care of her two daughters while she attended a women's retreat. She asked if I could help with household chores, like cooking, laundry, and light cleaning. Feeling honored that she trusted me, I agreed.

One evening, after tucking the girls in bed, I went downstairs to fold some laundry. The pastor was in the family room, resting in his chair. Soon after, I heard him asking if I could give him a shoulder massage. I did not think twice.

Moments later, the pastor turned around and started to kiss me. This sent me into a state of shock and confusion. *What the hell is going on here? How do I get out of this situation without making him angry?* I was frozen.

Seconds later, I felt his tongue in my ear, and I quickly pulled away and ran out of the house. Running down the road, I cried to God, "What is it about me? Why does this keep on happening?"

I ran for what seemed like miles, crying out to God. In complete exhaustion, I collapsed by the roadside. With my body shaking and my heart racing, I thought I was going to die. About thirty minutes later, I gathered my composure and slowly walked back to the pastor's house.

I walked into the house and went directly to my bedroom. With my thoughts racing, I could not fall asleep. In the morning, I knew I would have to pack my belongings and find somewhere else to live.

As I lay on my bed, I tried to figure out what *I* had done wrong, why *I* was responsible, and why it was *my* fault. Another thought was, *Why do pastors do this to me?* No matter how hard I tried, my father's voice kept telling me it was "always the female's fault."

When morning came, I realized I had nowhere to go. The only solution was to stay busy at work and study in my room. One thing was certain: I would avoid the pastor at all costs.

One day at work, I shared my recent experience with a female coworker. I told her about the wife's church retreat and what had happened with the pastor after she left. Without hesitation, she invited me to live with her. She said we could share the expenses. So I packed my belongings the next day and moved in with her.

Not long after the move, I received a phone call from the pastor's wife asking me why I had moved out. Not knowing what to say, I made an excuse. I told her a coworker had invited me to stay with her because it was closer to the hospital for me. Sharing her disappointment, she said she understood. She told me she wished she could have said her goodbyes instead of coming home and suddenly finding I had moved out.

After I moved in with my coworker, I felt a renewed sense of peace and contentment. I put what happened behind me and focused on my work and school.

Within weeks of my move, I found a new church to join. Considering my past two experiences with pastors, I needed to be extremely cautious in not developing any personal relationships with them or their families. Still, I needed to attend church and continue to grow my faith. If I lost this connection, Satan would win.

Getting Help

Although life seemed to improve, I still had bed-wetting problems. Knowing I had great health-care insurance, I sought professional help from a doctor at one of the local clinics.

After a series of appointments and tests, no medical issues were found. Although I was relieved, I was also disappointed in not finding the root of the problem. I was referred to a psychologist named Dr. Feldman. I was told he was one of the best in the field.

I was amazed at the doctor's understanding and empathy when I had my initial intake. I felt very comfortable, which made it easy to tell him my life story, starting from my childhood experiences through the experiences with the two pastors who had abused me. It was liberating to share my entire story. This was my first experience of many with a therapist.

In our discussions, he devised a plan to help alleviate my bed-wetting issue. I was given an electric rubber mat to plug in beside my bed, and it would have a buzzer that would wake me whenever I wet the bed at night. I was encouraged to drink as much water as possible beforehand and document the time and amount of fluids I consumed. I was then instructed to record when the alarm went off at night.

To my relief, the doctor encouraged me that most of my issues were due to stress and the abuse I endured in my youth. This was a relief to hear since I had put all the blame on myself.

The therapy I received from Dr. Feldman was very beneficial, alleviating my bed-wetting challenge by about 90 percent. I finally felt some hope for the first time in my life.

I'm Not the Only One

After a year of living with my coworker, she pulled me aside one day and told me she had something important to discuss. She continued by sharing that although she was a believer, she did not have time for church. After hearing what she said, I invited her to my church. She asked where I attended, and I told her. With some hesitation, she welcomed the idea of going to church together. Since she worked every other weekend at the hospital, she could only attend twice a month.

A few weeks later, my friend appeared sad and distressed. I knew something was wrong. In sharing this concern, she said she needed to tell me something.

She informed me that the church pastor had visited her about a month after she first started attending. She said the pastor hugged her and tried to kiss her. My eyes quickly welled up, and I felt tremendous empathy for her. I could not believe that a pastor had taken advantage of her too.

Although shocked and angry, I quickly put two and two together and realized these situations were never my fault. I immediately felt some relief. After all, she knew about my two experiences with pastors.

After listening to what she said, I knew I had to go to the church and tell them right away. I do not know what came over me, but it was easier to stand up for her than for myself. Perhaps it was because in my situation, I was told to keep it a secret.

I called the church to set an appointment to meet with the deacons. In the meeting, I explained what had happened. Surprisingly, they minimized the situation by saying it was my roommate's fault. They further instructed me not to speak to anyone about this. I left angry and horrified.

A few days later, the pastor called and wanted to meet with me. In the meeting, he denied any responsibility, claiming that my roommate had made moves on him. I was so frustrated by his lack of integrity being a man of faith. I abruptly left in disbelief.

It still amazes me that I did not turn away from God, given I was a new believer. Maybe it was because I was used to abuse and injustice.

Although my friend left the church, I continued to be involved, which helped grow my faith. Because I enjoyed singing, I joined the church choir. My hope also was to meet other single people.

A short time later, I noticed a familiar face sitting in the back row. Taking a cautious, discrete second look, I recognized him as a famous pastor from Nashville.

After a few years of attending the church, I began feeling lonely as I was not connecting as I had hoped. Frustrated, I went to one of the church leaders to express my concern. After careful consideration, he challenged me to develop a ministry for singles. Although flattered, I was scared. How was I to start a ministry for singles when it was hard for me to connect with others?

After reviewing the church population, I realized many single people were attending the church. With this new insight, I decided to take up the challenge and assemble a singles Bible study group. Doing this helped me gain a renewed vision and purpose by being in a leadership role.

DATING

As far as dating relationships went, they were virtually nonexistent. I went on an arranged date with a premed student once in college. We met at a coffee shop, talked for about five minutes, and realized we were not a good match for each other. We exchanged pleasantries and never saw each other again.

I realized I did not have the proper social skills and was all thumbs when it came to dating. I was timid and insecure when it came to the opposite sex. I wanted to be in a relationship with someone, but I was scared, knowing how hard it would be. In terms of sex, I was even more terrified of not knowing if I would like it or not. I knew one thing: I would not have sex before marriage.

I was determined that if I were to marry, it would be to someone who was a believer and attended a Southern Baptist church. There would be no compromising, and I was sure the probability of finding someone my age who fit those qualifications was low. Besides, I had finally come to a point where I was content with where I was in life, working in the medical field and leading the church's singles ministry program. Finally, I had a purpose.

CHAPTER 4

Dreams Do Come True

Dreams do come true for those
who do not give up.

—Unknown

Despite battling the shaming inner voices, I was content with life. After all, I had spent most of my life learning how to ignore the voices. I was good at it. Why change?

I worked full-time as a night-shift aide at one of the local hospitals. I continued taking classes part-time so that I could earn my nursing degree. I was active in church, singing in the choir, leading a singles Bible study, and trying to develop healthy relationships. Through all this, I felt God was helping me discover more effective teaching and leadership skills.

The singles group met each week for twelve weeks. The group had eight members who were mostly females. We discussed the Bible and how to apply its teachings to our everyday lives. We enjoyed spending time together, going to restaurants, bowling, and playing board or card games. It was a tightly knit group, and we enjoyed one another's company.

Not long after volunteering at the church, I received a call from the denomination's headquarters. They asked me if I would be on a committee organizing their first ever retreat for singles. Of course, I was excited and honored and said yes.

Over the next few months, we met to discuss plans for a November retreat. Fortunately, the denominational headquarters was in the same city where I lived.

After a few months of planning, I realized that I had a conflict with my school and the weekend of the retreat. I had a big anatomy and physiology exam on the Monday following the retreat. Because I had failed these two classes previously, I knew I needed time to study.

Knowing I could not reschedule the date of the exams or the date of the retreat, it left me only one option: to pack up my anatomy and physiology books and head to the retreat, knowing I would have to take every opportunity to study.

After arriving at the retreat center located in Southern Wisconsin, I went to the registration desk, registered, and dropped my luggage off in the women's dorm.

I went to the social gathering area and noticed a slim, handsome young man who was the center of attention. He had dark, wavy hair, dimples, and a mustache. Bolstering my confidence, I slowly walked toward him, keeping my distance because I did not want to be noticed. In other words, close enough to listen but safe enough not to be part of the scene.

Mesmerized by his good looks and his Southern twang, there was something special about him. We locked eyes, and he slowly walked over to me. After the usual pleasantries, he began to share stories about his recent mission trip to India.

Soon after, others joined in to hear more about his preaching experience. Everyone seemed very excited to listen to what he had to say, and I was no different. He seemed to be everything I had been looking for. Most importantly, he presented himself as a God-centered man.

FALLING IN LOVE

Not long into the weekend, the same handsome young man approached me and wanted to introduce himself personally. He said his name was Barry, and he lived in Mokena, Illinois. I told him my name was Melissa and that I lived in New Buffalo, Michigan. I also told him I was a nursing student.

Barry shared that he worked as a cook at a local restaurant and was also his church's music minister. Feeling intrigued, I felt a school-girl crush coming on.

During the singles retreat, the group had a couple of hours between guest speakers. Having time on our hands, the group decided to go bowling. Barry, being the gentleman he was, asked if I was going. I told him I would typically want to go; however, I could not because I had to study. He asked me what I was studying, and I told him I had an anatomy and physiology exam on Monday. He asked if I needed any help studying, and I said, "Sure." This was a new experience because nobody had ever put my needs before theirs. My feelings for him were intensifying even though I had just met him.

Studying with Barry helped and was filled with fun and laugh-ter. What made it fun was how Barry tried to pronounce the various names of the bone and muscle groups of the body. I hadn't laughed so hard in such a long time. Surprisingly, it helped me memorize the material for the test.

The weekend quickly rushed by as we tried to find a few min-utes to chat here and there. I do not remember much about the event or the speakers; I thought more about the thirty-one-year-old, good-looking Southern man who had caught my eye.

When the event ended, Barry approached me and asked if we could keep in touch. With blushing faces, we exchanged phone num-bers and addresses.

I was a schoolgirl with her first crush, and I left the event with anticipation. Barry exceeded all my requirements in a man. He was good-looking, charming, and respectful. He believed in God and was part of the Southern Baptist denomination. I was on top of the world. Who would have thought I would meet the man of my dreams?

A few days after arriving home, I received a phone call from Barry. He asked how I did on my exam, and I was excited to tell him I had passed. He told me he was happy for me and that I deserved the best. He continued by saying how fun it was to spend time with me.

The following week, Barry traveled the ninety-mile stretch from Illinois to Michigan to visit me. Since neither of us had much money, we spent our time walking around the city, going to parks, talking about life, eating at a fast-food restaurant, and laughing. Barry was easy to talk to and had a dry sense of humor, which I liked. As the day ended, Barry asked if he could kiss me. Feeling slightly embarrassed, I consented.

There was something special about my first kiss that I'd never forget. I remember having butterflies in my stomach and feeling a bit light-headed. My heart was pounding, and I felt my blood pressure rise and a burning sensation on my face. I was vulnerable. Although I did not know how to kiss, I assumed Barry liked it. Regardless, I felt respected and honored for having been asked.

My feelings for Barry grew as I was swept off my feet in ways I had never experienced. I could not believe I was falling in love so quickly; it was something I had not thought possible.

The Stars Were Aligning

I had always desired to be part of a Christian family. After a few visits with Barry, I learned that he came from a strong Christian family. His parents were avid church attendees who lived in a small town near Marriottsville, Maryland. His family seemed to be extremely close and very supportive. This was all new and exciting to me.

Barry had two brothers who lived close to his parents and grandfather. His grandfather was a retired boxer and preacher. I learned that Barry had earned a degree in pastoral ministry and sincerely desired to be involved in foreign missions. In addition, I learned that Barry had two uncles in church ministry who also lived in the Marriottsville area. I immediately gravitated to Barry's family. I was envious.

I felt that God was leading me to be a part of Barry's life. He did share that he was engaged once before but had to call it off because her parents disapproved of him, stating he was not good enough for their daughter. I felt sympathy for him and never questioned him further as it seemed to be a very dark time in his life.

Not long into the relationship, we began to talk casually about marriage. We often had our discussions walking through department stores and looking at household items and children's clothing. We talked about how many children we wanted, even considering the names we would give our children.

Six weeks after we met, Barry officially asked me to marry him. He proposed to me in the kitchen of my small efficiency apartment while eating a bowl of chicken noodle soup and a peanut butter sandwich. Immediately, I sprung to my feet and said yes! I was so in love with him and grateful that someone like him loved and valued me enough to want to marry me.

I was delighted when Barry told me he wanted to ask my father for my hand in marriage. I thought it was so sweet of him and felt deeply honored that he wanted to ask for my father's blessing. Although I was not sure how my father would respond, I respected Barry for wanting to ask him.

As it turned out, my father did not hesitate to consent but assured us that neither he nor my mother (she was not given a choice) had an interest in attending the wedding. I knew my father would respond this way, so I wanted to ensure that Barry knew this before asking my father for my hand in marriage.

After Barry received my father's blessing, we went to a Valentine's banquet at my church. Barry stood up from the dinner table and presented me with a beautiful engagement ring. I was so surprised and proud to share the moment with my church family. Everyone at the banquet appeared extremely happy, affirming we were doing the right thing.

Our love for each other was so strong we could not wait to get married. We quickly set a date in September, six months after our engagement. Another consideration for getting married so soon was to help offset our individual living expenses.

During this time, we wrote several letters expressing our love and devotion to each other. We made plans to visit every weekend by alternating who would drive the ninety-mile distance. I loved traveling to where Barry lived, especially since I knew this was where I would live after being married.

Barry and I had many conversations regarding our sexual values, and we both felt strongly about holding to our Christian morals. Our sexual commitment to each other did not last very long as we became sexually active without having intercourse; we saved intercourse for marriage.

As we began our sexual experience together, I was initially perplexed when Barry's hands went beneath my clothes discreetly when we kissed, unsure if we should be doing this. I quickly reasoned that it must be okay since he was a licensed minister and my fiancé.

Being concerned, I talked to Barry about our sexual behaviors. I asked if what we were doing was sinful. In a quick response, he assured me that nothing in the Bible mentioned what we were doing was wrong. Further, the Bible only addressed having sexual intercourse before marriage as a sin. Having trust in what he said, I believed him. He also assured me he would not have sex with me before marriage.

Being naive, I truly enjoyed his gentle, loving touch on my body. In the back of my mind, though, I questioned if what we were doing was appropriate and if our actions pleased God.

Looking back, I think I was in love with being in love since I had not experienced love before. I did not doubt that this was the man for me. Still, I wished we had taken more time to get to know each other and resolve our privately held issues. I also regret not spending time in premarital counseling, which could have helped us immensely.

Regarding premarital counseling, I did ask my pastor (the same pastor who made inappropriate advances to my roommate), but nothing ever came about.

As I remember, there was one elderly couple who attended our church who had concerns about my relationship with Barry. They discreetly asked if I would be interested in hearing what they had to say. Believing they had my best interests at heart, I agreed.

They shared concerns about how quickly we were getting married. They said they saw some red flags I should be aware of. They told me they were concerned about how Barry talked to me. I promptly dismissed their advice, thinking they did not know him as well as I did. I know now I was wearing rose-colored glasses and was not open to seeing anything other than what I needed to see—a perfect man.

From a very early age, the idea of getting married was a dream. Now the dream was real. I was so ecstatic I wanted to shout to the world, "I'm getting married!"

I thoroughly enjoyed planning my wedding. Although Barry's parents helped us financially, I knew I could not count on my parents for any financial support. It was hard for Barry to understand my parents' attitude, though he respected it. In the big picture, it did not matter to us as both of us had grown accustomed to living the simple life, with no frills and no elaborate material things.

As the planning moved forward, we both agreed to be married in my church by my pastor. We both loved how the church was set up, and Barry knew that I was extremely close to my church family.

Many of my church friends helped me plan the wedding. One friend helped me design the invitations, another helped plan the flower arrangements, and another volunteered to play the harp. Feeling blessed would be an understatement.

It was music to my ears to hear my friend play the harp. I never shared this hidden childhood dream with anyone, as I thought I would be laughed at if I ever shared it.

Because my father would not be walking me down the aisle, I asked an older gentleman I knew at church if he would be interested. With tears in his eyes, he said it would be an honor.

In deciding who would be my maid of honor, I thought of my roommate, who took me in when I did not have a place to stay. She, too, teared up and said it would be an honor.

Although Barry was encouraged to help with the wedding plans, he was uninterested. His only request was to have his father be his best man. Hearing this, I was inspired that he thought of his father that way. Part of me was jealous of his close relationship with his father.

Barry told me his family would travel from Marriottsville to share in the celebration. This would be the first time I would meet his family in person. Unfortunately, my family would not be attending. We were okay with this arrangement because we only wanted to celebrate with the most important people in our lives.

With limited funds, I found a beautiful, floor-length white wedding dress for less than $75. I also found an inexpensive veil to compliment the dress. I chose baby blue and white as colors for our wedding since Barry's favorite color was blue. I wanted to please him in every way possible.

Barry and I chose to write our wedding vows. Our vows expressed our love and admiration for each other. We were to honor each other's feelings, be patient and kind, and prioritize each other "until death do us part."

This was going to be the best day of my life. I honestly could not wait to be the loving wife of this handsome Southern gentleman. I looked forward to spending the rest of my life with him. I would finally have that perfect Christian marriage I so dearly desired.

All my expectations were met. We had just under a hundred people in attendance. Our wedding day was filled with sunshine and blue skies. It was picture-perfect in every way.

Our reception was held in the church basement, where we had blue punch and a beautiful three-tier wedding cake to share with Barry's family and our friends. After the reception, we were bombarded with rice as we ran to our decorated car as husband and wife. I was incredibly proud to be Mrs. Melissa Roberts.

CHAPTER 5

Dreams to Nightmares

My best dreams and worst nightmares
have the same people in them.

—Unknown

Married life began exceptionally well. We enjoyed spending time together, whether watching television, taking long walks, or playing card games. Our sexual intimacy was great too. However, it wasn't long before those internal voices of mine began to echo in my head, saying I was not worthy or good enough to be loved by someone, let alone be married. These demons were overshadowing my marital happiness.

I felt unsafe sharing those inner voices with Barry, as I did not want to take the chance that they might be right. So I came up with an idea: I decided to drop out of college, quit working as a nursing assistant, and become a full-time wife.

When I shared my idea with Barry, he supported the idea because that was what his mother did. Barry talked about how great it would be. Now I could care for him just like his mom cared for his father. He shared with me that he had the ideal family and childhood. He was very proud that I was willing to model our married life after his family.

Being a stay-at-home wife would allow me to take on side jobs such as babysitting or secretarial work a few hours a week to help with our finances. However, it led me to feel guilty. I felt guilty because Barry's mother never worked outside the home. I wanted to help out financially, but I was concerned that Barry would be angry. Surprisingly, Barry never objected as long as I was home when he came home.

Financial differences were never a big issue as we both subscribed to paying off our credit card debt each month. We resolved that if we could not pay our monthly credit card statement, we would not use our credit cards.

We agreed that eating out no more than once a week was essential to our budget. Because of our limited finances, eating out tended to be at fast-food restaurants. Although not the healthiest, it was a time together that we both enjoyed. Also, I did not have to cook, which to me was a big plus.

I loved being married, and I adored my handsome husband, perhaps not for the right reasons, but they were reasons nonetheless: one, I was a people pleaser, and two, I wanted a completely different marriage than my parents.

I enjoyed the attention I received being married. It was refreshing to have someone to share my thoughts or ideas with. I also valued the fact that I had someone to help with everyday decision-making. Best of all, I felt like I finally had someone who loved God as I did and also loved me. I was now living my dream of being loved by a God-fearing man. I felt life would be perfect from here on out.

It was a huge relief when I rid myself of my maiden name and most of my bed-wetting challenges. I now had a new identity.

Recalling conversations with my psychologist, he told me that adult bed-wetting often results from childhood trauma that has not been resolved. Although my bed-wetting was no longer an issue, other childhood voices began to arise in my mental chorus, shouting "I'll never amount to anything," "I'm not worth anything," and "Anything bad that occurs is my fault." To help quiet the voices, I became more involved in the church. Of course, staying busy did not resolve the problem; instead, it compartmentalized them in a tiny box deep inside me.

INSECURITY

I was becoming extremely obsessive about Barry coming home late from work, even if only a few minutes later than expected. I often imagined Barry being in a tragic car accident and that God would take him from me. I depended on him so much that I could not imagine life without him. Barry was the center of my universe, and every thought and action I had revolved around him.

I remember several occasions when he would come home from work, and I would lash out in anger because he was a few minutes late. I would shout out spiteful words to get his attention. I did not understand why he didn't call to let me know he was running late. I was overreacting, but I could not help myself.

Our sexual relationship was short-lived due to my pessimistic view of sex and those shame-producing inner voices. They constantly told me I was not worthy, leading me to experience our sexual time together as a "duty" rather than intimacy. Not long after, Barry began to express his frustration with me that he was not getting enough sex, even though we were intimate one to two times per week. Upon hearing this, I spiraled down into the abyss. On top of everything else I had to deal with, my sexuality was not enough to keep him happy and satisfied. Once again, my insecurities boiled to the surface, making me believe I was the problem and a failure.

I stayed very busy keeping the voices at bay. However, when we decided to leave the church three years later, I resigned from over fifteen positions I was heavily involved with. Staying busy with church activities became my religion to help curtail those voices in my head. No matter how involved I was, it never really silenced them.

As a result of leaving the church, Barry told me he sensed God was leading him to move to Marriottsville, where some of his family was ministering. Being a submissive wife and an avid people pleaser, I wholeheartedly supported the idea of us packing up and moving. Ironically, we both were sensing the call from God, and it seemed apparent that he was leading us to minister somewhere other than where we were living.

We made the move less costly by selling or giving away our furniture. With fewer belongings, we rented a small trailer and moved to Marriottsville.

Without knowing where Barry would work or where we would live, we set out on a new adventure without having any financial support. We trusted that someone in Barry's extended family would help us out.

As it turned out, one of Barry's cousins offered to let us stay in his tiny ten-foot-by-twelve-foot camper, which was parked in his backyard. Because it had no toilet or shower, we had to use the one in his cousin's house. Adding to the challenge, Barry's cousin had several children, so we did our best to keep out of the way.

Because Barry did not have a job, we let his family know he was interested in a pastoring position at a local church. Within two weeks, we learned of a church looking for a pastor. Barry's parents and his grandparents, who lived in the area, assisted us financially while Barry secured a pastoral position.

After much discussion and praying, Barry gave the church his résumé. He went through the interview process, which included Barry delivering a Sunday morning sermon. The church voted, and Barry became the new church pastor.

Barry's parents were thrilled since they (especially his father) had been pushing him to become a pastor for a long time. Being a family legacy, Barry was the only one of three who had attended seminary. It wasn't until years later that I learned it was more due to his father's pushing rather than Barry's desire to become a pastor. Regardless, everyone was overjoyed with my husband's new position as senior pastor.

PREGNANCY

My first pregnancy was relatively easy. The church was supportive as they threw me a baby shower. Although the church did not have a parsonage for us to live in, we found a small two-bedroom apartment less than a mile away. It was indeed a blessing after living in a camper for three months. It was also close enough for Barry to come home for lunch.

By the end of June, I gave birth to a six-pound, fifteen-ounce healthy baby girl. We named her Diane. After giving birth, I began to feel better about myself. I was a mother, and our baby girl was perfect in so many ways. This, of course, boosted my self-esteem. How could an unworthy person like me give birth to a perfect baby like her? Deep down, I felt I had finally done something right.

Although the church was supportive, many grandparent figures did not hesitate to advise us. We knew they meant well, but it was a bit intrusive. Barry and I took time to sit down and evaluate everyone's opinion. Because Barry was their pastor, we felt we were put in a catch-22. The catch-22 was that we would be upset if we followed the advice we disagreed with. If we did not follow their advice, then they would be upset. Given this dilemma, we had to painfully consider our options as we did not want to rock the boat. Regardless of our decision, we knew their advice was designed to help us as new parents.

The first few weeks of being a new mother were wearing on me. Diane tended to be fussy, as most babies can be, and I had no idea how to soothe her when she cried. I felt all alone and did not want to ask for help from the church; they were already too free with advice.

Adding to the stress, I did not want to ask for help from Barry's family, as they, too, were overly involved, just like the church. Given our options, we followed the church's advice with reservations.

The advice came from every direction, but all that was important to me was that I raised Diane differently than how I was raised. Knowing my family history, I was bound and determined to break the cycle of physical, verbal, emotional, and sexual abuse. Sadly, my family's abuse dated back at least two generations. I realized I needed to allow God in my life more now than ever if there was any chance of becoming a healthy mother.

Diane was less than a year old when I began to experience marital distance. Barry was busy pastoring the church, and I was hard at work learning to be a great mother. I started hearing more and more of those old familiar voices reminding me of the past. This time, they were echoing louder and louder.

The voices seemed the loudest when Diane was having her fussy times, and they shouted that I was the cause of her fussiness. With an already challenged marriage, I did not know what to do. After contemplating sharing this with Barry, I found some inner strength and asked him if he wanted to go to marriage counseling. Expecting to hear the word *no* because of our finances, I had prepared myself. Surprisingly, however, he agreed. I was relieved to finally get professional help to silence my inner voice and help our marriage. Fortunately, our denomination was very good at providing resources to help ministers and their families.

Every week, we would take Diane to our counseling appointments because we did not have a babysitter. Barry knew of my struggles with Diane, and he sat quietly while I shared my concerns with the counselor. I thought he was a very thoughtful and kind husband at the time.

However, I seemed to be the only one talking during our sessions. Barry just sat back and listened, never sharing about himself or the marriage. I was even more upset because he was not sharing his issues with the counselor. If he did not share, how could we work on our marriage together?

Shock and Humiliation

About six months had passed since our initial visit with the counselor when I received an unexpected phone call from Barry. I had just put Diane down for a nap and was looking forward to some downtime. Barry informed me that he had bad news. My mind began racing with thoughts of Barry in the hospital or that someone we knew had died.

He told me the police were at the church and that there was a problem. He explained that someone at the coffee shop next door to the church had called the police because they saw him repeatedly standing by an open church door, exposing himself, and masturbating. I heard the words *exposing himself* and *masturbating*, which nearly knocked the wind out of me. I started to feel light-headed, and the sound of Barry's voice grew fainter and fainter. It was as if everything stood still.

After a few moments, I came to my senses and quickly reasoned that there must be a mistake. Surely this could not be my husband. Barry would never do something like that. It had to be someone else.

As it turned out, it was Barry. Fortunately, the coffee shop decided not to press charges but strongly encouraged Barry to get counseling for his exhibitionistic behavior. The church immediately demanded Barry's resignation. Barry's sexual behavior left us jobless, shameful, embarrassed, and confused. I wondered why time in counseling did not identify any of Barry's issues. Strangely, I was not angry with Barry or our counselor.

Completed dumbfounded, I did not know what to say or do. We lived in a small town, and everyone knew everyone's business. *What will people say? What will people do? What will I do now?*

We continued counseling, learning that this issue occurs because of the occasional stressor's pastors experience. Not knowing anything different, I accepted this explanation. Looking back, I now understand how naive I was.

At the time, I thought it was best to be a good pastor's wife and support what the professional had told me. After all, who am I to question the professional? Ignoring my gut instinct, I did my best to support Barry during this very trying time. I even encouraged him to move past this tragedy and move on. Barry found a job as a meat slicer at the mom-and-pop butcher shop next to our apartment.

While trying to deal with all this, I would take Diane out for a walk in her stroller. Often, I walked with a dear church friend. During one of our walks together, my friend told me that the head deacon of our church had seen us walking together. She said the deacon believed that Barry's masturbation resulted from me not meeting my husband's sexual needs. I was horrified, and I did not know what to say. She also told me the deacon did not want her to associate with me. I immediately felt angry, frustrated, betrayed, and alone. My mind immediately returned to what my father had always told me,

"It is always the woman's fault if a man has trouble sexually." Even though I was angry at the deacon, deep down I blamed myself.

Despite what the deacon told my friend, we continued our walks together because she knew how much I needed her support. Looking back, I secretly harbored the blame for Barry's termination and felt guilty about what had happened. Since we accepted that the stress of pastoring a church was the cause of Barry's masturbation, his issue was never really addressed.

As life moved on, Barry continued his job while I spent most of the time sitting on the front porch, reading books, and watching over Diane. I still felt intense embarrassment and insecurity when people walked by, wondering what they thought or said about Barry and me.

SECOND CHANCES

We eventually found another Southern Baptist church to attend a few miles away. After a few visits, we became friends with the pastor and shared with him what had happened at our previous church. To our surprise, he was grateful and prayed for us.

After a few months of mentoring, Barry was asked to be an associate pastor. Barry was also asked to be in charge of the choir as the worship leader. Barry loved to sing and was thrilled. I supported Barry's decision and joined the choir. I never thought about what might happen if Barry got too stressed out.

Barry and I decided we wanted another child and stopped using birth control. It wasn't long before I learned I was pregnant with our second child. Since our apartment had only two bedrooms, we decided to find a larger place to live.

A friend from our new church had a mobile home that she decided to sell us. The arrangement was for us to pay the monthly land rent and utilities. Not having much money, we quickly accepted.

Because Barry made a modest income as an assistant pastor, he kept his full-time job. After all, we were going to be a family of four.

Our son, Jerry, was born a few months after our move into the mobile home. Life seemed to be going well again, and we were now living our family dream.

God gave us a second chance at a new church and location. Even though the voices of my past occasionally crept in, I was able to distract myself by staying busy as a mother of two.

About four years into Barry's mentoring by the church pastor, the pastor suggested it might be time for Barry to branch off independently. He showed us an interdenominational newspaper regarding a Michigan-based church starting a new church plant.

At the time, I was homeschooling Diane in her kindergarten year, while Jerry was busy being an active toddler. We prayed about moving as we looked at the area's demographics and what Michigan offered.

Praying together united us in at least going through the church's interviewing process. After being accepted by the church, we packed up our family and moved to Michigan.

Our move led us to live in a mobile home on a short-term basis until we could find a house. The Michigan-based church assisted us financially in helping us find our first home. We also received financial support for three years as we began the new church plant.

Within a year, I found my dream home. It had three bedrooms, two baths, and a large front porch. It was located on a beautiful large lot where our children had plenty of room to play. It had a sufficiently large structure designed to start our new church plant. Everything seemed in place as we began another new chapter in our life.

Not long after moving, I took a newspaper delivery job to help with the finances. Although our children were young, they enjoyed traveling with me, delivering newspapers. I continued working for a few years until both were full-time elementary students. I was impressed with the school system, so I no longer needed to homeschool.

Once Diane and Jerry were in school, I found a new job as a paraprofessional at the local elementary school. I loved the idea of being able to work in the same building where my children attended school. I loved my job helping to make a difference in the lives of young children. Barry supported me in working at the school because I would be available for our children in an emergency.

Although the extra income did help our struggling budget, I did not become a paraprofessional for the pay; instead, it was to be with the children.

STORM ON THE HORIZON

As the saying goes, "It won't be long before another storm hits us." Trouble began to creep in once again. A few church members observed that Barry struggled with motivation as we held church services in our backyard. As usual, I took on the responsibility of making things right.

I tried my best to support and encourage Barry. I made sure we had frequent sex. I tried to hide my worries and concerns behind my smile. I even tried to laugh more, to no avail.

Unable to make things better, I went to the pastor of our governing church, Barry's pastoral supervisor, and told him about our struggles. After consulting with him, he concluded that we needed to focus on building our marriage before trying to build a church. After hearing this, I felt so defeated, and those same old familiar voices shouted that it was my fault again.

I reasoned it had to be my fault, as I was the only common denominator causing Barry's pastoring and marriage failure. I heard the voices screaming that I should not be in the ministry, that I should not be married, and that I should not be a mother.

The voices were constant, and I tried to silence them by rehearsing that I was the best wife I could be. After all, I was doing the opposite of what my parents did because I knew yelling, name-calling, or throwing things was not how to react when tension builds. I cooked meals I knew Barry liked. I traveled to places Barry enjoyed. I even provided Barry with sexual intimacy, even though emotionally and physically, I was not interested.

Our children were struggling too. Jerry had bladder and defecating issues throughout his elementary and junior high years. We

71

took him several times to doctors, trying to understand his struggle. We even took him to a counselor to see if he could help explain why he was having these issues.

His bed-wetting and defecating challenges triggered me because of my own struggles growing up, and I did not want him to go through the same stress. The doctors could find no definable cause for his issues.

In her junior high years, Diane developed a hatred toward Barry. She and her father had enjoyed a close relationship in her younger years. With the onset of puberty, everything changed. It seemed that anything Barry did brought on a fit of anger.

Our daughter later got married at age nineteen. As tradition goes, Diane was to have her father walk her down the aisle. However, she insisted he would not touch her, hold her hands, or walk her down the aisle. To add further injury, the minister who married Diane told her she *had* to let her father walk her down the aisle. This resulted in her being furious with the minister.

To this day, I have tried to talk to Diane about why she has such a hatred toward her father, which leads me to believe something happened. With no closure, I am unsure what to do as my daughter reiterates she does not even know herself.

I became increasingly good at hiding my pain in public. I was adept at pasting on a smile, and I knew this was because of years of doing this as a child.

Although I did get angry at times, I did my best to hide it. I guess you could say I learned to be passive-aggressive. Whenever Barry said or did anything that triggered my anger, I would suppress my frustration and act as if everything were fine. I masked my pain with a smile.

Uncontrolled Anger

It was Super Bowl Sunday, and the outdoor temperature was around twenty-five degrees. I remember there was about a foot of snow on the ground. Out of nowhere, my anger erupted like a volcano. Barry opened the freezer door to our refrigerator, and the frozen food fell onto the floor. He put everything back except a pound of ground sausage that had rolled under the kitchen table.

After he had finished picking up all the frozen food, he went outside to shovel snow on the driveway. When I walked into the kitchen and found the sausage roll under the table, I immediately felt something snap inside me. In the blink of an eye, I ran outdoors without wearing a coat and threw the sausage at him; it hit him in the chest. I jumped on him, hitting him endlessly. I remember screaming at him. I am sure it was a Super Bowl Sunday that our neighbors would never forget.

After my unforgettable rage, I went back into the house and sat in a state of shock. It reminded me of my father's behavior, whom I never wanted to be like. To make matters worse, I remember Barry telling me how he enjoyed how I jumped on him and raged at him, making me angrier, and I never processed what he meant by that.

After that, I harbored my mounting anger toward my husband. I must have done a great job because we were often told that we had a great marriage. Of course, this was by people who did not really know us.

Before we were married, Barry commented on how he never had any close friends. About twelve years into our marriage, I understood why. Barry always struggled to initiate conversations unless it was about himself or sports. When it came to sports, he could quote any baseball, football, or basketball stat, even naming all the players in each sport.

However, when it came to identifying his feelings, let alone expressing them, very few words would be spoken. I saw tiny glimpses of this at the beginning of our relationship, and sadly, it became more prominent as time went on.

Barry never found it easy to develop deep working relationships with his peers. Developing meaningful relationships was complicated for him, whether within the church or elsewhere. If anyone knew sports, he was all over that. My anger grew toward him as he would dominate conversations, not letting others share their thoughts or opinions. This was an ongoing grievance.

Barry focused on matters that were important to him rather than what was important to me. It became increasingly evident that no matter how I tried to let him know how I felt, he seemed not to care. I found it to be extremely puzzling. He could remember the baseball stats from yesterday's game but not remember what I shared about my feelings.

To help him, I tried putting important dates and events on the calendar. I tried to schedule meaningful conversations, but nothing seemed to work. I was often left feeling devalued, unworthy, and angry.

We never talked further about the Super Bowl Sunday debacle. It was not something my husband wanted to discuss.

Conflict Avoidance

Barry came from a family where conflict was never dealt with, and I learned more about this from him as time went on. Barry shared that he, too, had to bury conflict under an imaginary rug. Admittedly, I did not know how to change our marital dynamics.

Somehow, I mustered up the strength to confront Barry. I struggled to evaluate the pros and cons of facing him over weeks of nonstop indecisiveness. If I wanted a deeper connection with my husband, I realized I had no choice but to confront him.

I asked if he would be willing to see a Christian counselor concerning his emotional intimacy challenges. I told him I desired a deeper relationship with him. To my surprise, he graciously said yes. I immediately sought a Christian counselor from a nearby city as our community had none.

Barry started going to counseling every week. Occasionally, I was invited to join him, discussing what he was learning about himself. This was new, as the focus had always been on me, not Barry. For me, it was a breath of fresh air.

As his counseling progressed, it did not continue to the point of making any significant, long-lasting change. I became increasingly aware that Barry was good at telling the counselor what he wanted to hear and knew how to get the counselor to like him.

This would become apparent when we would get back in the car and drive home. Barry would resume his old ways. When I voiced my concerns, he would shrug it off, saying I was too hard on him.

After a few more sessions with the counselor, Barry came home saying the counselor wanted me to join him during his next session. Knowing this was my best chance to call him out, I agreed.

I shared with the counselor what I was experiencing when we drove back home from our sessions. I further shared my concerns about Barry's lack of emotional attunement and continued distancing behaviors.

About midway through our session, the counselor asked me about my childhood. He suggested I see him individually to work on possible unresolved issues. My immediate response was to scream. I was shocked by his request and felt angry and betrayed.

After a while, I calmed down, but I quickly surmised that Barry's covert, manipulative plan was about getting the counselor to see that I was the problem, not him.

I could not believe Barry would turn the tables on me by having me go to counseling. What just happened? I thought Barry was going to counseling because he wanted to work on his interpersonal issues, and now he had me going. *What the hell?*

I now see that Barry's counselor identified what I did not want to see. I refer to him as the first "kick butt" counselor who did not sugarcoat what I needed to face. It was my first step on the road of healing, which took over twenty years of hard work.

After months of individual and couple's counseling, I discovered something on our home computer. While reading my emails, I noticed an unfamiliar icon and clicked on it. To my horror, a picture of a man's penis appeared. After recovering from my shock, I confronted Barry. He quickly denied knowing anything about it. He suggested that maybe it was our son, Jerry. I screamed. He was only nine years old, for heaven's sake.

Barry continued to blame Jerry as he was using the computer to play games. After hearing this, I got up and went to confront Jerry.

Jerry, of course, denied knowing anything about how the image got there. I believed him.

This led me to conclude it must have been Barry. Why would my husband want to see another man's penis? The thought left me feeling sick to my stomach. My mind searched frantically for answers. I wanted to say it was a mistake, but I couldn't.

I tried hard to deny what I had discovered. I wanted to believe Barry because I was his wife, and I wanted to believe only the best when it came to my spouse. I had to find out how that picture got on the computer. After all, images do not show up out of the blue.

Immediately I scheduled an emergency couple's session with our counselor. After much discussion, Barry admitted that it might have had something to do with him "accidentally" opening a pornography email. It did not take much for our counselor to conclude that our marriage had a deeper issue.

The counselor suggested that we might need a "therapeutic marital separation." I thought this idea was somewhat drastic, but we both needed physical, emotional, and relational space from each other, so we agreed.

Barry moved out, finding a room to rent for the next three months. Living separately, we continued our individual and couple's counseling.

Admittedly, this was very hard as I learned how I had taken Barry for granted. We had been married for almost seventeen years. Diane was thirteen, and Jerry was ten. Even though our two children were basically good kids, I found it challenging to parent them alone.

Although Barry did his best to provide financial support during our separation, being the sole parent was still challenging. On the positive side, I learned about the many challenges of being a single parent. Perhaps less important than parenting alone was trying to keep up with all the household responsibilities. Thank goodness both Diane and Jerry helped as best they could. Regardless, it was a heavy responsibility.

One of the biggest disappointments during our marital separation was with our church. I felt abandoned and shunned as they held the position that no matter the issue, no marriage should ever separate, even if it's therapeutic marital separation from a licensed professional.

I remember sitting down with my pastor and explaining what my marriage was going through. Of course, this was not new to him, as he was already aware of our struggles. Regardless, I received his message that a marriage should never separate, even under a counselor's supervision.

About three months after our separation, Barry and I met with the counselor and discussed reuniting. Although I never got any closure on how the image appeared on our computer, I concluded it must be just as Barry said: he had clicked on some pornographic spam.

Having a three-month separation helped me learn more about myself and my marriage. The bottom line was, I wanted to remain married to Barry.

Barry and I discussed what the pastor had said and concluded it was time to look for another church. We both agreed that our new church must be biblically focused and sensitive to marriages today.

Not knowing how his family would respond because they came from a strict Southern Baptist background, we still knew what was best for us. Upon sharing this with our counselor, he mentioned that we might want to check out his church.

We visited the church a few Sundays later and felt welcomed and loved by everyone. To our surprise, we even knew some of the people who attended. Soon after, we met with the pastor and shared our story. It was a welcome relief to share and not be judged. He assured us that the church would come alongside us and help.

CONTINUED PAINS

Our life together was off to a new start once again. Things appeared to have settled down not only in our individual lives but also in our marital life. I was once again excited about our future together, and I became involved in the children's activities at the church while Barry was busy working.

Although Barry did not continue counseling, I did. I wanted to work on resolving my family-of-origin issues, my struggles with negative-thinking patterns, and my bouts of depression. Admittedly, I was scared. Although there were still issues concerning Barry's memory and inability to deal with our marital problems, I had to focus on myself.

Along my journey of healing, I was growing spiritually. I started to notice Barry was not the spiritual leader of the home that I needed him to be. I made all the decisions, especially regarding our children's spiritual growth, leaving me as the spiritual leader.

This left me feeling emotionally and spiritually distant from Barry. I continued immersing myself in raising the children, investing time at my job (which I enjoyed immensely), and taking a leadership role in the church.

Barry appeared comfortable working at his job and watching sports on television. We occasionally did activities as a family, but it was getting more difficult as our two children became teenagers.

Our sexual intimacy was at an all-time low. I repeatedly tried to talk to him about how I was feeling and told him I was unhappy, saying it was too routine. To help mix things up, I suggested we schedule our sexual intimacy time on the calendar. I thought that having a plan would help us prepare.

Many times, after intimacy, I would cry silent tears, unable to understand why. I thought it was all because of my brokenness. I tried to give Barry what he needed the best way I could, but my heart was not connecting with him.

Occasionally, I encourage Barry to join me in my counseling sessions. However, whenever we went together, he only talked about how I was not giving him enough sex. In our sessions, Barry always said the right things, promising to be more communicative and honest with his feelings toward me. However, as usual, he did not follow through.

Driving back home was all too familiar—just another letdown and disappointment. I felt utterly discouraged and hopeless. As a result, I gave up on having Barry join me in further counseling sessions. My husband had no issue because he thought I was the issue. I was dying inside, and I felt so hopeless.

I was coming to the end of my rope. I was closing down, giving up on any hope of Barry opening up to me. I was emotionally beaten down and failing miserably, with no end in sight.

Barry began sleeping downstairs on the couch, and I was sleeping upstairs in our bedroom. We both used the excuse it was because of his snoring. Although not the best, it was better than what I had witnessed in my parents' marriage.

Occasionally, I would invite Barry to sleep with me, which occurred bimonthly. Given our marital dysfunction, I knew it was too big to address alone, as I was struggling to heal my own wounds, let alone heal the wounds of the marriage.

I remember having bizarre dreams of Barry standing in my bedroom doorway, and I thought nothing of it until I saw a dark image at the door one night. Knowing it was Barry, I asked him what he was doing, and he said nothing. Not long after, I discovered he was masturbating while standing in the doorway.

I was scared and felt violated. Now my bedroom was not even a safe place. After much discussion, Barry told me I was not supposed to see him there masturbating. *How despicable,* I thought. This left me feeling hurt, confused, and angry. What I thought were nightmares turned into reality. As a result, I did not trust him. I struggled each night trying to fall asleep, wondering what I might wake up to.

Pondering why he would do such a thing, I could not come up with a plausible answer. The only conclusion I made was that it must be somehow my fault. After all, the common denominator was me, and my rationalization was that I was not giving him enough sex.

I felt broken and ashamed. Inside I was furious but felt unjustified to blame him. I also felt angry about what he did but was upset with myself for not giving him what I thought he needed. I was so confused.

I had to look for another counselor because my current one had moved to another state. Fortunately, it did not take me long to find one. My new counselor suggested I meet with him weekly to start.

Once he knew more about me and my story, I could schedule with him biweekly.

Knowing there was a lot of hard work ahead, I was committed. I was tired of having those negative-thinking patterns fill my head with toxicity.

We began by talking about the recent event regarding Barry. I felt so embarrassed sharing that my husband had been masturbating at my bedroom door at night. The response I received from him was highly confusing. There I was, sharing intimate details of what my husband had been doing, and he had the nerve to tell me it was no big deal. He told me it was normal to masturbate in front of each other. I was appalled.

He continued by saying Barry had every right to do what he did. To make matters worse, the counselor also stated that there was nothing wrong with viewing pornography as long as we both agreed. I told him I never was asked, nor had I agreed. I could feel my blood boil, and I was livid, to say the least.

In sharing this with a few close, trusted friends, they said they suspected that Barry had a pornography addiction. I was dumb-founded. How is it that everyone else knew but me? I was sickened by the thought of pornography because I witnessed firsthand what it did to my father.

Being confused, I started to second-guess myself. I reasoned, given my history, that maybe pornography was normal and that mas-turbation was okay. I was now questioning my beliefs about sex, leaving me utterly lost.

In desperation, I reached out to my pastor and his wife. Since Barry and I had known them for about eight years, I felt comfortable sharing with them.

I remember sitting in their living room, telling them what had happened. I told them about Barry's sexual behavior, what he was doing at night in my bedroom doorway, and our lack of sexual inti-macy. I also shared what my counselor told me about Barry's right to masturbate and view pornography. Adding to my confusion, they were both adamant that I should not hold back any sexual intimacy from him, indicating I was the one to blame. I was devastated, and the depth of my despair ran deep.

I never anticipated they would blame me for Barry's behavior. They quoted scripture and gave me their "biblical" advice. All I wanted to do was curl up in a ball and cry. I panicked and wanted to disappear from life. I felt broken and lost.

After leaving and driving back home, I continued sobbing. I prayed and journaled, asking God to help me in my hopeless situation.

I contacted my counselor a few days later, letting him know what I felt. He suggested I talk to my family doctor. However, I was not particularly eager to take prescription medications but knew I might have to. After all, I knew I was emotionally worn down and in a very dark place, causing panic attacks to be my new norm.

Before I called my doctor, my panic attacks became more severe. One night, I woke up feeling prickly and numb on my right side. It felt like I was having a stroke, and I thought I would die. I went to the emergency room.

After arriving, I was evaluated by the emergency room physicians. They could not find anything medically wrong. Within a few hours, I was sent home with directions to contact my primary physician for a follow-up.

My primary-care physician suggested that I take antidepressant medication. Being one not to take medications, I reluctantly agreed. Unfortunately, the panic attacks continued, so I went online and looked for ways on how to handle my panic attacks. What I learned was how important it was to control my breathing when I sensed a panic attack coming on. I learned to take slow, deep breaths until my sense of panic resolved. I also prayed, which helped. Within a few days, my panic attacks ended.

I knew the stress of my marriage significantly impacted the quality of my mental health. Being on antidepressants, praying, and continuing to work with my counselor was a life changer.

Forecast—Cloudy with Rain Showers

The following two years were a blur. Our children graduated from high school, and Diane got married, as I previously mentioned. Both children continued to have an estranged relationship with their father. I knew this was not my fault; instead, it was Barry's, due to his inability to connect with his children, let alone me.

During the next several years, Barry and I worked with two different counselors. It was difficult because each counselor we saw told us that Barry was too hard to work with. Both reported that Barry was not doing the work required to help our marriage. This left me feeling hopeless and powerless.

Barry's memory kept worsening, so we had him evaluated twice for Alzheimer's and dementia, but nothing was diagnosed except for severe depression. As a result, Barry was under the care of a psychiatrist who prescribed several medications. Unfortunately, his condition worsened, and the medicines increased his anxiety and confusion.

Occasionally, during the night, I would hear Barry moan loudly downstairs. The following day, I would ask him why he was moaning, and his response was, he did not know what I was talking about. Being defensive, he would accuse me of being overly dramatic. Second-guessing myself, I chalked it up, believing it must have been a bad dream.

Days later, I heard the same moaning noises coming from downstairs, and I knew I was not dreaming. I confronted Barry, and he finally confessed that he had been masturbating in front of the computer and television. He claimed it was no big deal. His response was nothing new, as I had heard this from him all along.

I was furious yet scared. My thoughts were about who I could talk to and who would understand. This left me feeling stuck because I did not know where to turn and feared being told once again it would be my fault.

I prayed fervently, asking God what I should do. I knew something had to change, or I would go completely insane.

Feeling desperate, I took the chance and called my pastor's wife. This was the same pastor's wife with whom I had shared my marital concerns with, only to be told it was my fault. I didn't care because I was desperate and needed someone to listen. When I called, she agreed to walk with me and let me vent my heart. I knew I was taking a considerable risk of rejection.

She listened and remained respectfully silent as I shared my story. When I was finished, she took me by the shoulders and, with her face six inches from mine, told me I needed to kick Barry out of the house immediately. I was shocked. Not long ago, she and her husband had reprimanded me for not giving him enough sexual intimacy, and now she was encouraging me to throw him out.

Prayers answered! I quickly remembered what I had previously prayed for. Without a doubt, I knew it was God. My only concern now was, how would Barry respond?

When I arrived home from the walk, I immediately sat Barry down and calmly informed him that he had a problem and that he desperately needed to find help. I told him he could no longer stay in our home until he got the proper help.

Barry admitted he knew he had a problem but did not know where to go for help. After spending several hours researching and making phone calls, we finally settled on a place that seemed like a good fit.

The place we found focused on adult men with addictions. They stated they were not working with men with sex addiction but were willing to take on Barry.

Barry called and made arrangements with his place of employment, and he got a leave of absence with six months' pay. Admittedly, the program was costly, but we felt it was the only chance to get help for Barry's emotional and sexual problems.

Within a few days, Barry packed his belongings and left for his six-month program. Although I would live alone for six months, it would be worth it if it helped Barry. After all, the children were out of the house, and I only had to care for myself.

Although I did not know what tomorrow would bring, I knew it had to be better than what I was experiencing. At times, my anger crept back in, but I reminded myself things must get better.

I had doubts about whether this would take care of Barry's emotional problems or not. I learned the medical director there took Barry off all his depression and anxiety medications as they wanted to start with a new baseline of care.

The program focused heavily on scripture study. The men in treatment did construction work for the program director to help keep them busy. They reasoned that scripture reading and hard work were the two cures for treating addictions.

I received weekly updates and learned from the director that Barry was becoming a model student. I was further told that Barry was now free of his addiction. Although I had my suspicions, I was encouraged. After all, the men there were constantly monitored throughout their six-month stay.

After prayer and discussion with close friends, I decided that Barry should live alone for six months posttreatment before moving back home. I had to see for myself if Barry indeed had overcome his addiction. As I later learned, however, the treatment facility focused not on his emotional challenges but on his sexual behavior.

Upon graduation, the recovery program held a massive celebration for all their recovering men. The director met me before graduation to inform me of Barry's remarkable success, and I quickly told him I was not feeling the celebration myself.

I shared with the director that I needed Barry to live six months independently to ensure his recovery success. The director responded by telling me I was making a horrible mistake, and he further told me I had an unforgiving spirit.

Not knowing where my confidence came from, I responded without hesitation, saying I strongly disagreed with his critical judgment. I further told him that forgiveness is a process rather than an event, and I also stated that trust is what I needed more than anything else. Anyway, I attended the celebration with the support of a couple of my female friends.

Barry did find another place to live on his own, and he could go back to work at his place of employment without any issues. During our separation (post-inpatient recovery), Barry and I occasionally went out together to talk and share what we were learning about ourselves.

Although I agreed to meet with Barry for date night, it was tough as there was no restoration of trust. I would be hypervigilant, trying to catch any sign of concern.

Through careful observation, everything appeared to be going well. He was doing everything I asked, which Barry never had an issue with. He seemed compliant but never learned to share how he felt. This left me feeling fear and doubt about our marriage.

I felt worried and anxious as we approached the end of our six-month separation. I knew the feelings of panic far too well, and I did not know if I was genuinely ready to take him back.

Because of everything I had been through, I felt God was leading me to join a ministry that focused on helping other women in similar situations. As a result, I enrolled in online classes to teach me how to help others who had been abused. I was fortunate as the church provided an office to work out of. Having a passion for helping other women, I gained a reputation for caring for others. Finally, I had found something I felt I was good at. It clarified how to use my past, find a purpose, and use it to help others.

While we were on our six-month separation, my pastor called me into his office, wanting to talk. Not thinking anything of it, he said that if I did not let Barry come back home in a few months, I would not have an office to work in. He said Barry had successfully jumped through every hoop I gave him, and it was time for me to let him come home. He said that I needed to show him God's grace. I did not know what to think. Was this God speaking to me? I was feeling intense fear, and I thought I was being manipulated. Should I turn off my gut instinct and do as I was told? I felt a lot of turmoil. I knew I wanted to continue to help abused women. Having no choice, I let Barry move back home.

GROUNDHOG DAY

Barry was overjoyed to move back home, and I tried to be happy for him, but I felt so much fear. To help me process my feelings, I had a close female friend with whom I felt safe to share. She attended Barry's recovery graduation program with me, and her support was a blessing.

I reached out to her often after Barry moved back home because I did not have closure in understanding why Barry was sexually acting out. After all, if he did not understand what caused him to act out, how could he be recovered? Consequently, I never knew the reason why he behaved that way. All I could do was have a wait-and-see attitude. My belief was, in time, the truth would be revealed. And it was.

About six weeks after Barry moved back home, I received a phone call from the local library. One of my distractions from dealing with reality was reading. I developed a relationship with the local librarian because of my frequent trips to the local library.

The librarian called, asking if I could come down to the library. I said yes, thinking she had received a new book I might be interested in reading. Since the library was less than a mile from home, I decided to walk.

When I arrived, two library aides immediately escorted me to the back of the library. One of the aides told me they had a problem with Barry. She informed me that Barry had come in earlier to use the computer. She said they both noticed he was carrying a jacket, covered his lap, and saw a wet spot on his trousers when he stood up. After he left, they investigated and discovered he had been browsing some pornography sites. I was in shock, but I maintained my composure.

She said they thought he was masturbating while watching pornography. They knew we had been through some tough times in our marriage and thought it would be wise for me to know. How could he do this again, let alone after recovery? In public, again?

Thanking them for letting me know, I left the library and returned home, sobbing. I called my support friend, who, with her husband, had helped mentor us after Barry returned home from our separation.

I had no idea how to approach this and desperately needed her help. Since it was a short time before Barry came home from work, we decided for my friend and her husband to come over and help me confront Barry with this news.

I needed their support as I knew I could not face Barry alone and didn't trust myself. While waiting for him, we prayed, asking God for guidance.

When Barry arrived, he was surprised we had company. I asked Barry to sit down, and I told him about my trip to the library. Barry immediately became angry and denied anything had happened. He was outraged that the library aides would make such accusations.

At that moment, I started to second-guess myself. Had I misunderstood what the aides had told me? I asked my friend if she would walk to the library with me to double-check what I thought I heard while her husband talked privately with Barry.

When my friend and I entered the library, we asked the librarian aides to tell us what they saw, and they both repeated the same story. My friend asked them if there was any way they might have made a mistake, and both emphatically claimed it happened just as they described.

We slowly walked home, praying that her husband could get Barry to confess. When we arrived home, Barry firmly stood his ground that he never acted out in front of the library's computer. I told him that if he came clean now, we would work through the problem together, but our marriage would end if I found out he was lying. Barry vehemently replied he was telling the truth.

The next day, Barry went to the library and confronted the two librarian aides. Barry said he was angry and frustrated by their accusations and demanded an apology, which they refused to do. Barry stormed out in frustration.

I did not know what to believe, but I knew God knew the truth, and my prayer was that he would reveal the truth to me. I resolved that I had to accept things as they were for now and move on, even though it was difficult.

I went back to living life behind my smile. Barry continued to work, and I went through my usual routines. I continued to struggle with trusting my husband and felt extremely uncomfortable and unsafe being in the same room with him. We continued to meet with my friend and her husband as they mentored us.

Barry and I still slept in separate rooms as I could not bring myself to sleep in the same bed with him. I communicated that I no longer wanted to be sexually intimate.

I continued in a marriage I no longer valued. Barry repulsed me, and I felt neither passion nor compassion. I questioned everything about my marriage. Profound anger became my new norm.

I held on by learning how to be patient and wait for God's perfect timing. Eventually, the truth would be known. My focus was to survive day by day. Although Barry and I continued going out now and then, it wasn't easy, but I knew I needed some normalcy.

About two months after the library incident, I finally got the truth I was looking for. Barry and I were at a restaurant, and Barry commented he had something to share with me that would probably make me extremely upset. I became instantly anxious as he rarely had much to say to me. He broke down and told me the library incident had happened just as they said. He then apologized for lying to me. He also admitted to acting out during his stay at "inpatient," stating he had not been sober. I was shocked, disgusted, and simultaneously relieved because my gut instincts were validated. He had been lying all along.

After hearing this and his plea for forgiveness, I told him I was done. He tried to convince me to give him one more chance, but I had already decided. I told him I could not live with him like this anymore and would not tolerate his lies and dishonesty, period.

I continued telling him this was not what I had signed up for or dreamed about. I told him I did not know what my tomorrow would look like but knew I would survive. I told him that if I had known the truth all along, I might have been able to support his and our recovery steps. However, living life without truth was no longer an option. I told him it would be a certain death sentence for me and my marriage.

SECTION II

Facing a New Reality

CHAPTER 6

Confronting Denials

Denial keeps us blind to those things
we don't want to see because our minds
don't feel we're ready to handle them.

—Ken Seeley

What the hell just happened? I was still attempting to comprehend what Barry had confessed. Hearing the truth was like getting hit by a truck. My body wanted to curl up in a little ball and not be seen.

I knew separation was inevitable. Deep down, I was a bit frightened of what might lie ahead, but I knew there was a need for change. I needed this for my sanity. Regardless, I still felt uneasy, and I was now preparing myself to make a drastic change.

What I had been doing over the years was not working, and I knew I had to put on my big-girl pants and face reality. So many times I switched back and forth, wanting to deny what happened but wanting to face the truth.

Internal battles challenged my thinking as I was always taught to think the best about others. But a more significant need was to know the truth, and I had learned that truth was more important than my comfort.

My thoughts rolled back and forth, and I felt I was on the edge of insanity. My prayer to God was for him to reveal the truth, no matter the pain. The more I focused on what I thought were the issues, the more I saw our marriage falling apart like a crumbling brick wall.

I tended to see cups half empty rather than half full. As my thoughts raced, I was on the edge of having a nervous breakdown. My gut said something was wrong with Barry, but on the other hand, I thought maybe it was me. It was always easier to blame myself.

As time passed, I struggled with focusing on anything in my daily routine. I often forgot names, where I was going, or what I was doing. I felt like I was living in a fog and could not understand what was happening to me. Work at school was difficult; even taking a breath was difficult. I felt so lowly and broken.

AGREEMENTS AND DISAGREEMENTS

When it came to drinking alcohol, Barry and I agreed that it was unhealthy for both of us. As previously mentioned, I grew up in a home with alcohol abuse and knew I could easily fall into it.

Barry grew up in a family in the Deep South who were Southern Baptists, and their belief system forbade the use of alcohol. Barry had been raised never to enter a restaurant that served alcohol because it was said to be evil. Regardless of the influences of our past, we were both aligned when it came to alcohol use.

During Barry's rehab, I surrounded myself with supportive church friends who helped both Barry and me during our marital challenges. Many of them drank wine, which made me rethink my personal views of alcohol. Part of me desired the freedom to choose but was also scared I might become like my father.

My more significant concern was what God would think of me if I started to drink alcohol. After all, if I drank, God might be mad at me, and that was the last thing I wanted.

After lengthy discussions with my friends and searching scriptures about alcohol use, I decided to make a personal decision that would allow me to drink. Drinking alcohol had to be monitored and controlled. After all, I wanted to live life not fearing what others would say or what God might think.

I learned that Jesus and the people of the Bible had partaken in wine as it was the custom of that period. I discovered in my search that scripture often spoke of drinking alcohol in moderation.

After some praying, I let myself join my friends in enjoying a glass of wine now and then. I promised myself to have boundaries that I would have no more than two drinks. It was a new experience that I enjoyed in moderation. I also knew that Barry would not be happy with my change in beliefs.

We were having dinner together at a restaurant one beautiful spring evening. I thought it would be a good time to be honest and explain what I had learned during our separation. I shared with him about rethinking my view on alcohol. I shared with him that many of our friends at church drank in moderation.

Barry became quiet and stared at me like I had gone crazy. He then said he was displeased with my decision and feared I would become an addict like my father.

Upon hearing this, I could not understand why someone who was struggling with addiction himself had the right to accuse me that I was going to be an addict by drinking one or two alcoholic drinks. I was furious. I felt overwhelming guilt because I was trying to choose to become the person I wanted to be and not let others decide for me, especially Barry.

After prayer and discussion with my supportive friends, I decided to give myself the freedom to have a glass of wine within strict guidelines.

Respecting Barry, I never drank in front of him, and I believe this became a start in allowing me to be me. It also helped me address the fear of worrying about what others might say when they disagreed with one of my decisions. Slowly I became the person I wanted to be, having choices and freedoms.

In evaluating my love for Barry, I had thought of coming up with a list of a hundred reasons why I did, and I thought this might help me know my true feelings for him.

It did not take much effort or time to come up with the list, which gave me a glimpse of hope that our relationship was not as bad as I thought. After completing and tweaking the list, I presented it to Barry on Valentine's Day, hoping it would be the game changer in our marriage. Barry glanced over it, thanked me (at least he showed a bit of appreciation for my effort), and shoved it aside. Bewildered, I felt hopeless and worthless.

We never talked about issues, so this was no different, and life went on as usual. Occasionally, I would take brisk walks in our neighborhood, listen to Christian music, and pray. It would be something I found very therapeutic, especially when life was stressful.

Typically, when I left for a walk, Barry would play games on the computer. Occasionally, when I returned from walking, I would find the front door locked. Time and time again, I would have to knock on the door for Barry to let me in. When I would ask why he had locked the front door, he explained he did not know I was out walking, so he locked the front door. Feeling irritated and mad, I accepted his explanation rather than get into a fight. I thought it was just easier to let it go.

In my frustration, I shared this with my counselor and pastor. Surprisingly, both brought up the possibility that Barry was likely viewing pornography while I was out walking. To protect myself from what they were saying, I slipped into denial, discounted their reasoning, and dismissed what they were saying.

After everything Barry and I had been through, I further reasoned, *Why would he lock me out of the house and view pornography?* Surely, it must be something else. I could not bring myself to believe my husband was looking at porn while I went out on a walk.

I do not know why, but I kept living in denial, believing sex addiction happened to others, not my husband. Rather than accept Barry as a sex addict in denial, I again took on the blame for our marital struggles.

After Barry's confession regarding the library incident, I knew I had chosen to overlook all the red flags over the past thirty-plus years. I so wanted to believe the best in my spouse. It was easier to blame myself because I knew my faults and was constantly reminded of them through the voices in my head.

For some reason, I was able to catch myself from continuing to live in my denial, and I saw it was time to face reality and take action to bring about healing. In truth, my gut was telling me that I was not the cause of my inner turmoil. Rather, it was the voices of my past. Breaking through denial, I knew I had to face reality again.

A New Plan

Living a life filled with dysfunction and confusion, I learned the value of journaling to help me process my thoughts and feelings. Often, I would journal to God about the pain I experienced, pleading for him to provide relief and healing. I also thought of writing to Barry's addiction to help process my emotions. Below is the letter I wrote:

Dear Sex Addiction,

How dare you! How dare you enter my home and create the pain and distrust you have done. Many preachers and ministry leaders have spoken about you, but you were distant then. I empathize with those affected by you, but you were not a part of my life. I heard stories of how you create pain and chaos in families, but I did not know until now you were in mine.

I am astonished that you have been a companion in our home for many years. You slowly invaded my home almost thirty years ago, and I did not know you were there.

I did see signs of you but refused to believe. I wanted to believe the best in my husband, and I wanted to trust him because I thought I was supposed to do that. Much pain was experienced because of you, but I did not know you were the root of the problem.

I have attempted to make all the right choices, even seeking Godly counsel over the years, but you already had your tentacles within my home unbeknownst to me. I take comfort that none of the counsel was in vain because I have been made stronger in the Lord and wiser because of it. You will not win in this. I can assure you of this.

You have created false guilt within me numerous times over the years and caused great shame over the last thirty years for Barry and me.

At the moment, I feel like you have taken a knife and sliced my heart in half, leaving it wide open to bleed where I cannot hide it. The pain is unbearable, which you have caused. Sometimes I cannot breathe, and I must remind myself to breathe and live through the next moment, the next task.

Many people have tried to tell me of your presence in my home, and I heard the many lies you created. Regrettably, I helped you exist because I was living in denial.

I have witnessed my husband's withdrawal and anger, but I did not realize you were the source and how crafty you were.

When suspicion was at its greatest, I prayed to my Heavenly Father to reveal the truth, despite the pain I experienced. It is true what the Bible says in John 8:32 (NLT), "And you will know the truth, and the truth will set you free." Even though the truth is painful, it is also freedom. Freedom from the lies and hold you have had in my home.

I have news for you, my enemy. My Jesus is much stronger than you. You may have slowly snuck into my home, but my Master is stronger than you.

I may feel weak, and I may feel immense pain from what you have done, but my Jesus has assured me that I am not alone (Deuteronomy 31:8), and he promises healing for my hurting heart (Psalm 34:18).

Jesus is my Defender, my Stronghold, and my Rock (Psalm 18:2), and as long as I can focus on him throughout this situation, my Jesus will win. He sees my tears (Psalm 56:8) and holds me in his arms as I walk through this season of my life. I may not know what tomorrow looks like, but my Jesus and I will not allow you to win without a fight. So there, Sex Addiction, to hell with you!

From a determined Christ follower

As I finished writing this letter, I knew life had to be different. I knew I had a long journey if I wanted to heal. I needed to confront my denial and start living in reality, knowing what was real and true. I remember promising myself: no more avoiding reality, no more making up excuses, no more living in fear.

CHAPTER 7

Setting Boundaries

Love yourself enough to set boundaries.
Your time and energy are precious, and
you can decide how to use them. You
teach people how to treat you by deciding
what you will and won't accept.

—Unknown

I viewed boundaries as a line separating properties, either a fence or hedge line. If there was no visible line, there were no boundaries. Having to think about relational boundaries in a relationship was a foreign concept.

The issue I saw with setting boundaries was that it would cause others to dislike me, and this would create a catch-22 scenario as I needed to be approved and liked by everyone.

As embarrassing as it was, I thought it was my duty to please my husband in every way and always think positively about him, no matter how hurt or uncomfortable I became. As it turned out, I lost my identity, which developed into a sense of hopelessness.

When I attempted to set boundaries in our marriage, I quickly made excuses for Barry, letting him off the hook. Some of the rationales were that he was fighting depression, that he had interpersonal challenges and the onset of early dementia, which caused him to forget quickly.

How could I set a boundary with someone who had so many challenges? That appeared so cruel in my mind. Furthermore, at the beginning of our marriage, we promised never to mention the word *divorce*. So I concluded that I would live with this for the rest of my life.

FINDING A CERTIFIED SEXUAL ADDICTION THERAPIST

Finding a CSAT therapist who was Christian was fortunately easy. My support friend and her husband told Barry and me they knew a therapist we should check out.

As it turned out, they referred us to John, a CSAT Christian therapist specializing in marital issues, sexual/pornography addiction, and partner betrayal trauma. The only problem was that his office was ninety minutes away. We knew no other therapist with credentials like this near us, and we both felt this was our only hope. Although we had gone to many different therapists, we knew this one was our last straw.

The process was intense. Barry would travel ninety miles twice weekly, once for his therapy and the other for his weekly recovery support group. He also had to establish an accountability partner with whom he had to report to daily.

Barry's therapist put him through a series of assessments to help evaluate the severity of his addiction and interpersonal challenges.

Eventually, Barry had to complete his therapeutic disclosure to me, admitting all his acting out sexual behaviors with his therapist present. He also had to evidence the truth by taking several polygraphs throughout his recovery program.

Having Barry take a polygraph yearly was one sure way of knowing the truth as he was a great deceiver. From start to finish, Barry was in recovery for over five years.

Barry did well in the first couple of years of recovery and did all that was required. Occasionally, he and I would meet with his therapist to discuss his progress and see if I had any questions or concerns.

Life appeared promising for the most part, except my trust level was still low. As we entered the third year, Barry proclaimed that he would not go through another polygraph, violating one of my boundaries. I told Barry I could work through the addiction issue but would not tolerate lies. After completing two years of intense therapy, we hit a brick wall.

I knew I had to do something differently when Barry confessed his lying. I had read many books about boundaries, and I was under the guidance of a good counselor specializing in addiction and the betrayal trauma it can have on the partner. I knew I had to begin setting boundaries, for if I did not learn, I was afraid I would lose my sanity, at least what was left of it.

In counseling, I learned that relational boundaries help separate one person from the other to help distinguish their unique identities and individuation. I learned there were personal, physical, emotional, spiritual, and sexual boundaries that needed to be known to oneself. My counselor said it best, "Boundaries help define who we are and who we are not."

As a child, every aspect of my life was violated by not having boundaries. I grew up believing my body was my father's property. My father slapped, pinched, grabbed, and even intrusively showed me things I should not have seen. I viewed this as him liking me and giving me approval since it was more emotionally painful when he ignored me and gave me the silent treatment.

My father often called each of us names that were demeaning or cruel. We all learned to accept his abusiveness. If we protested, things would get worse without warning. Because we did not know about having personal boundaries, we had to take whatever he dished out. *Boundaries* was a term that had no reference.

Even as a young adult, I had no concept of having personal boundaries. As stated previously, two pastors crossed personal boundaries with me, but I allowed such violation because that was how I coped as a child.

In an unhealthy way, a part of me felt accepted and liked when others crossed boundaries. I remember feeling confused, knowing that "something" was wrong, but I struggled to say no. Although I was able to get out of these situations, I felt I was doing something wrong by getting up and leaving; it was so confusing.

As a middle-aged adult, I experienced another pastor who would jokingly ridicule me in front of the church congregation. People would laugh when he made hurtful remarks about me. I thought if others were laughing, then it must be okay.

Another way he would ridicule me was by spitting on his finger and sticking it in my ear, even in front of the deacons. Being the brunt of his jokes made everyone laugh. Although it did not feel right, I went along with the joke.

Feeling upset that I was often the brunt of his jokes, I made an appointment to tell him how I felt. After sharing with him, he said I needed to be thick-skinned, and I felt completely dismissed. Extremely upset, I left and could not get past the thought that, somehow, I was wrong. After all, he was a man of authority. Never again did I approach him about his continued behavior.

SETTING BOUNDARIES—BLUE, RED, PURPLE PEOPLE

To help develop healthy boundaries, I first needed to learn how to evaluate my family and friends based on their relational closeness relative to being healthy or unhealthy.

My therapist had me work on identifying by name my family and friends. He started by having me draw three concentric circles. He then asked me to list the names of people I usually associated with, beginning with those who had the closest access to my life and who best knew me. He reminded me to make sure I listed all my family and friends. Any names of family and friends I wrote in the inner circle were the ones who had the closest access to knowing the real me (see figures 1, 2, 3).

I started by listing the names of people closest to me relationally by writing their first names in the inner circle. These were the people who knew me the most.

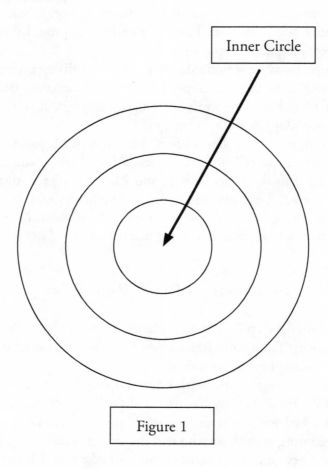

Inner Circle

Figure 1

Moving to the middle circle, these were the names of people who are the next closest to me relationally. Unlike the inner circle, these people had the nearest access to me, not as close as my inner circle but those next closest relationally.

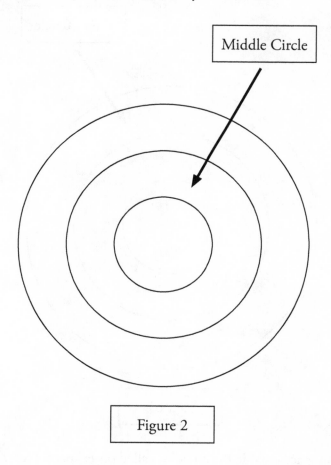

Middle Circle

Figure 2

Last was the outer circle. These were the names of people who were the next closest, not as close as the middle circle but still relationally close.

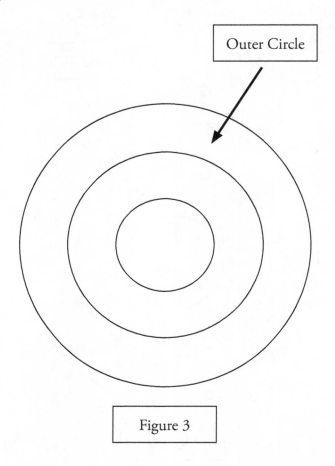

Figure 3

The space outside the circles is called outer space. Here, I wrote the names of people I knew as acquaintances, coworkers, and people I knew but were in the "outer limits" of having a relationship with me. After filling in all the circles with names respective to my relationships with them, I used the following color codes to help identify who was blue, red, or purple.

Starting with a blue marker, I was to circle any person's name that fits the definition of a blue person (see pg 105) regardless of where I placed their name. Circling a person's name entirely in blue meant they fit the description. However, if they only fit the description some of the time (50 percent or so), I would circle only half of their name in blue (half circle).

Blue. These were highly trustworthy people, family, and friends I could call anytime or confide in. I could tell blue people anything, and they would not judge or criticize me.

Blue people were considered to be the best cheerleaders in life. They were honest and supportive, wanting me to be my best. They would never take advantage of me nor put me in harm's way. They were the healthiest people I knew, regardless of where their names were placed on the paper.

Blue people, however, would never fear confronting me if I was doing something wrong or making a poor choice. In other words, they were not afraid of calling me out.

Next, using a red marker, I would circle any person's name that fits the definition of a red person (listed below) regardless of where I placed their name. Circling a person's name entirely in red meant that they fit the description. However, if they only fit the description some of the time (50 percent or so), I would circle only half of their name in red (half circle).

Red. These are seen as toxic people. They would gossip or be harmful to me. They would often try to tempt me or take me for granted. They were the ones who found pleasure in making fun of me. They were emotionally off-balance and would lash out in anger when they did not like my resistance to them.

I learned to recognize red people simply by their inability to nurture and support me in ways I needed. My therapist strongly encouraged me to avoid these toxic people because they would hinder my healing and maturity. Unfortunately, I learned I had many red people in my life.

Next, if I circled anyone's name in half blue and half red, they would be known as purple people (see pg 106).

If anyone's name was not circled with any color, it simply meant that I had not yet evaluated them. In other words, it was possible that my paper might not have everyone's name in a color.

Purple. The last color my counselor said I needed to evaluate was purple. He asked me to look at whom I had circled red and blue. If I found anyone's name half red and half blue, they were known as purple people. I learned I had to be extremely careful of purple people because they could appear highly trustworthy one moment and turn against me the next.

To help me understand this, my counselor equated it to a box of chocolates. "You never know what you are going to get," according to Forrest Gump's mother. They are unreliable and unpredictable and can resemble a chameleon, sometimes supportive while other times unsupportive. These were the people I had to weed out of my life.

I was encouraged to identify where the blue people were on the diagram, and if they were not in my inner circle, I needed to learn how to bring them closer. After all, they represented the best support system I had in life.

I also needed to identify any red and purple people on my diagram and consider removing them from anywhere within at least the inner and middle circles. If any person's name were a noncircled color, they would have to be evaluated as either blue, red, or purple before I let them relationally close. Being assertive was a challenge as I tended to be a private person who would put on a smile and hide the pain I experienced on the inside.

Admittedly, I struggled with this because my upbringing had deep roots in confusion about right or wrong. I was taught never to share my struggles or challenges; if I did, I learned it was a sign of weakness. Showing any sign of weakness would mean I would be hurt.

As I began to practice communicating my feelings with friends, I found the strength and encouragement to experience that it was safe to be vulnerable.

Nonnegotiable Boundaries

Regarding boundary violations, my therapist encouraged me to consider having nonnegotiable boundaries. Establishing nonnegotiable boundaries meant I needed to know the immediate consequence if breached. If a nonnegotiable boundary were violated, there would be no discussion, second chance, or debate about what had happened. This gave me an awareness of what I would not tolerate, period.

I remember coming up with two nonnegotiable boundaries. The first was that Barry would pursue healing through therapy with a licensed therapist specializing in addictive behaviors. He had to see a certified sexual addiction therapist (CSAT) and follow everything required.

The second nonnegotiable boundary I had was that Barry would have to complete a polygraph any time I asked, no questions asked. If either of these nonnegotiable boundaries were violated, I would pursue a divorce, which I did not want to do. Still, I knew I had no choice but to follow through if my boundaries were violated.

ANOTHER RELAPSE

Within a few months, Barry confessed to lying about his sobriety. Although it was hard to hear, I was happy I did not have to exercise my nonnegotiable consequence of divorcing him.

Barry's recovery continued for another couple of years. I still struggled to trust him even though he was doing everything as required. I knew I had been down this road before, and the outcome was always the same. He knew how to work the program while living in denial and deception.

Everything stopped in the fifth year of Barry's recovery program because he was lying through omission. Lying through omission meant he was not telling me the whole story but rather only parts of the story. This was a deal-breaker that pushed me over the edge. I was now confronted with having to pursue a divorce.

After praying and consulting with my therapist and close, supportive friends, I knew I would not accept lies, slips, or relapses. I would no longer tolerate Barry's dishonesty. I was done with my roller-coaster marriage. Having been married for thirty-five years, it was sad to see it end. My childhood dream was shattered. Living in a state of lies, deception, and deceit was unhealthy for me. Divorcing my husband was one of the most challenging decisions I had ever made.

Even though my nonnegotiables were being violated, I had to learn the importance of keeping them. Although not yet an expert, I was getting much better, remembering the words of my therapist, "Boundaries define who a person is and who they are not." Not having boundaries caused me never to know my true self, and not knowing Barry's boundaries put me at risk of not knowing the real person I had fallen in love with. My mind quickly raced over to where I was going to live. The mere thought was overwhelming, plus I needed to know that I would not be blackmailed (like I was by the pastor) if I was the one to leave.

Since I was on a meager yearly income, I listed my needs and wants. First and foremost, I needed to bring my little fur baby (my dog) since he was therapeutic for me. I desired a two-bedroom home to have my grandchildren over. I also wanted to live in an area where I would not be afraid of the neighborhood. I took these items to prayer before God and waited.

Another boundary I set was to be financially independent of Barry, which was extremely scary since I was on a low income. Barry had made some choices in his addiction that could have easily resulted in legal implications. I did not want my finances or name to end up in the legal system.

Again, after praying and consulting with my therapist and friends, I pursued a legal separation. I worked with a lawyer friend who attended the same church I attended. It was important to me to ensure he would be fair to both Barry and me and have a biblical viewpoint on life.

I did not want to divorce him but rather give him a chance at recovery since he saw a Christian counselor specializing in sexual addiction. In some odd way, I thought I would not have to divorce him if he fully recovered.

Again, I needed to protect my name and what little finances I had control over, but I did not feel released from the marriage.

Besides, the label of "divorce" was stigmatizing and was a title I was unprepared for.

It was a short time before the word got out. The school secretary informed me that she knew of an apartment that would be available in three to four months. I learned I was welcome to bring my fur baby, and it had two large bedrooms and was located in a home next to a doctor's office in a safe location. I also learned the apartment required no initial deposit, no deposit for having a pet, and was only $350 a month. It fit my budget perfectly and was everything I had prayed for.

The only hurdle was that I could not move into the apartment for three to four months. Having to wait, I had to be patient and find peace in God's care. This was a challenge for me as I had a deadline to meet.

A day or two later, I received a phone call from my mentor expressing concerns for my emotional well-being. She and her husband offered to let me live with them until my apartment was ready. I quickly accepted and moved my belongings and my dog in with them. For the first time in a long time, I felt I was on the path of safety and stabilization. My fear and uncertainty were still present, but I was with people who cared deeply for me.

Even though I was in a safer place, I had to exercise a few other boundaries between Barry and myself. Since I felt some guilt, I consulted with my trusted friends.

One boundary was not to be in Barry's presence unless it was with my counselor. Barry was manipulative and played on my vulnerabilities by complaining about how inconvenient life was for him. Often, he had me second-guessing my boundary.

Thoughts ran rampant through my mind, such as *Is this something a Christian would do?* or *Can he emotionally survive on his own?* A part of me felt like he needed me to help him survive. *Great,* I thought. Now I was becoming codependent, as if I did not already have enough to deal with.

I knew any boundary would be challenging for Barry, and I would feel the effects of his dislike of my new healthy boundary and be tempted to compromise.

OFFICIALLY ON MY OWN

After moving out from my mentor's home, I discovered I had to make a few boundaries with myself. Initially, I took very few belongings from the marital home since I did not know what to take. I was overly concerned about Barry's anger if I took something I should not have taken.

Sometimes I had to return to the marital home to pick up more things. I would do this when Barry was at work. Whenever I went back, I found myself playing "detective." I would review his checkbook, recovery workbook, journals, or mail to ensure he was sober.

My sneaky behavior disgusted me, and I knew this would only add to my craziness. It did not take long to realize how this added to my stress, fear, and insecurity.

I thought about what boundary I needed to protect my mental health. After consulting with my counselor and friends, I established a boundary never to enter our marital home alone since there was a strong temptation to snoop. I learned to be content with what I already had. I discovered that most of the time, I didn't need the item as much as I thought.

CHAPTER 8

Successes and Disappointments

It does not have to look magical or pretty.
Real healing is hard, exhausting, and draining.
Let yourself go through it. Don't try to
paint it as anything other than what it is.
Be there for yourself with no judgment.

—Unknown

When I finally decided to file for a divorce, I wanted to ensure it was not out of anger. I recognized that I was struggling with letting go of my dysfunctional marriage and trusting God. Oddly enough, for some reason, there was a sense of comfort in living in a broken marriage. Living in brokenness was what I had been used to all my life, and stepping toward healthiness was a frightening thought. However, I had no doubt that God was releasing me from my marriage and wanting me to work on myself.

Eventually, I had to find some furnishings when I moved into my new home. I took a few things from my marriage: a spare bed, a rocking chair, pots and pans, a small television, and a dresser drawer set.

Because there was more that I needed, I received help from the community I was now living in. I was overwhelmed by all the support I received. I had never experienced an outpouring of love and care like this before.

After a life of being married, I now found myself living alone. Having to make everyday decisions was scary. It was a great relief having my fur baby, Ali, with me during this time of transition.

Because Barry handled all the finances and home repairs, I had to learn this independently. This left me having to lean on my faith that God would care for me. I no longer had Barry to bounce ideas off, so my supportive network became my family when making significant decisions. Looking back, I can see how God provided me the much-needed support.

I loved the idea of Barry going to John, our therapist, because I wanted Barry to get "fixed." It took only a few sessions before John requested that I meet with him individually, which surprised me. My thought was, *Oh, crap, here we go again.* I had thought the therapy was only for Barry; I was not the one who was struggling with sex addiction. In addition, I had not realized that John also specialized in betrayal trauma, which partners experience. After my initial hour session with him, I finally felt validated. John evidenced an understanding of the addiction and how it had caused so much confusion, pain, fear, and anger. It was a breath of fresh air, knowing that, finally, someone got it.

Not long into my sessions, John informed me that I was most likely experiencing complex post-traumatic stress disorder (C-PTSD) resulting from abuse from early childhood experiences.

What Is C-PTSD?

Note: The information below is not for treatment or self-diagnosis of PTSD or C-PTSD but for general information use only!

Complex post-traumatic stress disorder (C-PTSD) is closely related to traditional post-traumatic stress disorder (PTSD) but may have additional symptoms. Complex PTSD can happen if a person experiences repeated trauma over a long time.

PTSD, on the other hand, is a disorder that can develop after a person experiences a traumatic event (typically a single event). Both can result in symptoms lasting over months or years.[1]

Symptoms of C-PTSD

In addition to all the core symptoms of PTSD—reexperiencing, avoidance, and hyperarousal—C-PTSD symptoms generally also include the following:[2]

- *Difficulty controlling emotions.* It's common for someone suffering from C-PTSD to lose control over their emotions, which can manifest as explosive anger, persistent sadness, depression, and suicidal thoughts.
- *Negative self-view.* C-PTSD can cause a person to view themselves in a negative light. They may feel helpless, guilty, or ashamed. They often have a sense of being completely different from other people.
- *Difficulty with relationships.* Relationships may suffer due to difficulties trusting others and a negative self-view. A person with C-PTSD may avoid relationships or develop unhealthy relationships because that is what they knew in the past.
- *Detachment from the trauma.* A person may disconnect from themselves (depersonalization) and the world around them (derealization). Some people may even forget their trauma.
- *Loss of a system of meanings.* This can include losing one's core beliefs, values, religious faith, or hope in the world and other people.

---

[1] Medical News Today, accessed March 14, 2023, https://www.medicalnewstoday.com/articles/322886#what-is-complex-ptsd.
[2] Verywell Mind, accessed March 14, 2023, https://www.verywellmind.com/what-is-complex-ptsd-2797491.

All these symptoms can be life-altering and cause significant impairment in personal, family, social, educational, occupational, or other important areas of life.

My struggle was that I did not know what normal was. Even though I was challenged by being triggered by unknown reasons, I just learned to cope. Little did I understand the complexities of my early childhood abuse. It was such a relief to have a label and some verification of the pain and turmoil I was experiencing.

SUPPORT GROUP

One of John's recommendations to help me heal was to attend a group designed for partners of sex addicts (betrayed partners). The group met ninety minutes weekly—the support group consisted of partners of varying ages and walks of faith. I knew I had to join as I felt alone and isolated, and being around other partners gave me a sense of understanding and validation.

I was excited to join this group because I could now share my experiences with others who would understand and not judge me, partners who desired to know me and who could relate to the experiences I was having. I now had a voice and an audience who truly cared about me.

I was heartbroken to hear the stories of the other betrayed partners, as the stories were similar to mine. I was taken back by the range in their ages—some were in their mid-twenties, others in their late sixties.

I always believed Barry chose pornography because I was not pretty enough. As a child, my father consistently reminded me how ugly I was. Listening to how the other partners had felt the same way, I immediately recognized that it had nothing to do with my looks; it was all about Barry's choices.

It was a relief to have a support group where I could vent weekly and process what I was experiencing, even though it was a ninety-mile drive. As a group, we were able to be an encouragement to one another. I knew this was just what I needed—being around others who understood.

HEALTHY SELF-CARE

The first focus of my healing was the importance of developing healthy self-care. Healthy self-care included a healthy diet and exercise, and I also learned the importance of getting restful sleep each night. Knowing the importance of adding exercise to my daily life, I started walking a mile or two daily, regardless of the weather outside, with my dog, Ali.

I valued being among my support network and partner group, which helped me be accountable for my healthy self-care. I did not realize how withdrawn I had become being married to Barry. So much of it was because I felt I needed to be at home to "take care" of him.

Although we did go out, it was very infrequent, mainly due to Barry's interpersonal challenges. I became hypervigilant about what he might say or do. Consequently, it became easier just to stay at home.

To stay active, I would make it a priority to connect with my girlfriends. We would have coffee together, watch a movie, or attend a Christian concert. It felt so freeing to have these socializing activities, as Barry and I did not spend time with others socially.

Several times a year, a friend and I would travel a few hours away to walk the shores of Lake Michigan. I found walking along the beaches very relaxing. In some odd way, it gave me the strength to find balance in my healing journey.

TROUBLE AHEAD

A friend of mine and her husband had taken up bicycling a few years prior when I was still married. I certainly was not a bike rider by any means and had not ridden a bike since I was a little girl. As it turned out, my friend's husband had a twenty-one-speed men's bike they were not using anymore, so they offered it to me. I decided to try it.

It took a while to get used to the bike, but I was determined to make it work. With determination in my spirit, I rode with my friends for twenty to thirty miles. As I rode, I felt so free and empowered. My self-esteem began to increase.

After mastering my skills, I would often ride when I came home from work. There was one beautiful path close to me, and I thought I would try. It was a lovely spring evening, and I felt confident pedaling at a moderate speed. However, riding on the path, a low-hanging branch caught me by surprise, and I quickly swerved around it.

Unfortunately, my wheels slipped from under me, and I fell heavily onto my right side, with the bike on top. As I attempted to move, I felt an excruciating pain in my right hip and knew I was in trouble. Fortunately, I had a small bag clipped in front of my bike with my cell phone in it. With great effort, I reached into the bag and dialed 911. After I called for help, I also called my friend Lynn, who lived nearby.

It was not long before the ambulance and my friend arrived. The paramedics had to hike a quarter mile with a gurney into the woods to rescue me. After they loaded me into the ambulance and transported me to the hospital, I learned that I had a circular fracture of my femur and that it would require surgery to repair the damage.

With all the physical abuse I had been through, this was the first broken bone I had ever experienced. I had to wait two days before surgery, leaving me in excruciating pain.

After surgery, I learned I had two metal rods inserted—one in my right femur and the other in my right hip. It took me about eight weeks of recovery, which appeared daunting since I lived alone.

Not being able to get around, a friend of mine had me stay with her and her family for two weeks, which was challenging since I did not like to depend on others. After two weeks of being taken care of and receiving in-home physical therapy, I went back home to finish my recovery.

At this point, I was dependent on a walker to get around. Not thinking ahead, I had to figure out how to use the bathroom, given it was on the second floor of my apartment. Since I could not walk upstairs, I bought a bedside commode and set it up in the spare bedroom.

Thank goodness I had a dear friend from church who came over several times to empty my bedside commode in the upstairs bathroom. To think there were people out there who would do something like this for me. So many friends came out to help. I remember feeling emotionally overwhelmed due to the outpour of support I received.

Within three months of the accident, I started getting back on my bike and riding. On one particular day, when I returned home from a short ride, I noticed a bike at my front door. *Who left their bike at my front door?* I thought. When I went to investigate, I saw a handwritten note that read that the bike was for me. Someone had gifted me with a new bike. It further stated that I should ride a smaller women's bike as it would fit me better. I was so overjoyed with excitement and appreciation for someone thinking about me. About six months after my accident, I could ride up to seventy-five miles in one trip. It was a time of celebration.

THERAPY WITH JOHN

One of the tools I had been focusing on in therapy was expressing my emotions. As a child, I was often ridiculed or slapped if I showed any positive or negative emotions. As a result, I learned to shut down any feelings I felt, thinking that punishment would come. It took a lot of work to feel safe to share, but I learned how to let myself feel without fearing retribution.

Allowing myself to feel is still a work in progress. I still struggle to cry when someone is emotional or going through some sort of physical pain. I admire people who can easily cry when watching a movie or are being moved by a great church message. I feel this part of me is still fractured.

117

The Little Girl Inside

In therapy, I learned that I struggled with the little girl living within me. I viewed "Little Melissa" as a stinky, weak, ugly girl. I did not like her because she chose to tattle on her siblings and did all she could to be loved and earn her father's favor. I gave Little Melissa all the labels her father and schoolmates gave her. My hatred for her was so severe that it was difficult even to view a picture of her.

EMDR Therapy

To help me see this little girl for who she really was and not the girl I grew to despise, John suggested that I might benefit from a psychotherapy called eye movement desensitization and reprocessing (EMDR) therapy.

EMDR is a psychotherapy that helps heal the symptoms and emotional distress resulting from disturbing life experiences. The goal was to heal from my various traumas.

I had lived all my life up to this point genuinely believing "I am worthless," "I am ugly," and "I don't belong," all of which were repeatedly said to me by my father.

These beliefs controlled my daily life. EMDR helped me change my inner beliefs to "I am worthy," "I am a beautiful creation," and "I do belong." EMDR helped significantly in creating positive shifts.

Before EMDR, I was triggered by my negative cognitions daily. It could be as simple as something a person would say or even a tone they would use that created a negative memory (trigger).

Working in a school, I often got triggered by how a parent or a teacher spoke harshly to a child, reminding me of how my father often talked to me.

When I heard car tires squealing, leaving the school parking lot, I became triggered due to the memories of my father's weekly drunk-driving episodes.

When living in my apartment, my neighbor often had her boyfriend over to spend the night. Although very amiable and quiet, some nights, her voice became loud, filled with colorful words of profanity. This triggered me due to my father's use of shouting profanity. This trigger affected me so severely that I would curl up in bed like a little ball, fearing my father would come in and hit me.

When her boyfriend became angry, he kicked down her front porch railing. This reminded me of hearing my father throw things around the living room. Being triggered, I was too frightened to call the police.

EMDR therapy was something I wanted yet feared as it brought me back to those memories I wanted to bury and hide. I knew that if I wanted to change, I had to find the strength to endure.

At the end of my EMDR, John would utilize grounding techniques to help quiet down my nervous system. He would also tell me that it was very likely that for the next twenty-four to forty-eight hours post-EMDR, I might reexperience body and emotional disturbances. He continued by saying that if the disturbances became too intense, to give his office a call, and he would help me through them. Knowing this, I would arrange my EMDR therapy before the weekend or take a day off afterward.

With John's gentle guidance, I was given some practical techniques to help with the aftereffects. Utilizing deep-breathing exercises and grounding techniques was very effective. Because of the trauma's depth, it took me about two years to make significant progress.

Part of the struggle was that I never acknowledged my feelings as a child since that was how I survived. However, to be healthy, I needed to address those feelings and allow "my younger and older selves" to heal. Admittedly, I resisted the EMDR process for several months, delaying my healing.

Once I decided to embrace the therapy and not fight it, I made significant progress. In addition, once I decided to release myself from Barry, it freed me to work on my healing.

After six years of EMDR therapy and having a praying network of friends, I no longer experienced symptoms of C-PTSD. In a comparably short time, relative to living a lifetime of triggers, I was a free and healthy woman! There are no words to describe the freedom that

EMDR gave me, and I was no longer haunted by daily triggers that could bring me to my knees in fear.

Although I experience minor triggers occasionally, I can now brush them off and not let them have any power over me as they had in the past. I no longer fight with the labels tattooed in my brain; instead, I know who I am. I am loved. I am a precious child of God, the Creator of the universe.

As a result of therapy, I learned to love and embrace the Little Melissa buried deep inside me. I realized she had to do what she did to survive, and she helped make me who I am today. I have come to accept, love, and embrace her as a healed part of me.

"Dear Dad" Letter

Although my father passed in 2012, I was still haunted by his beyond-the-grave voice. During one of my sessions with John, he suggested that I write a letter to my father. With some hesitation, I followed his encouragement. The following was the letter I wrote in my journal:

Dear Dad,

I am writing to tell you I have received freedom from my Heavenly Father and am now experiencing independence from the bondage you held me in. I understand you were also in bondage with your father, but I will no longer allow that to excuse your behavior.

I have allowed you to give me a false identity. I am not stupid, no good, a piece of trash, or ugly but a wonderful creation of a God who loves me wholeheartedly!

I will no longer allow myself to live in fear of you. You have hurt me for so many years, and no longer will I allow you to continue to damage me.

In so many ways, I was not allowed to be a child because of your way of parenting. You treated me like a piece of shit at times, which I have allowed to carry over into my adult life.

No longer will I allow you to have that control over my life. You have abused me emotionally, physically, mentally, and sexually. Still, I am choosing to believe that I am not broken, defective, or damaged because I am a daughter of a wonderful and loving Father who is glad to choose me as his own.

No words can adequately describe your behavior choices and their terrible effects on me. I struggled with physical activities because you imprisoned my activities throughout my childhood. I have been laughed at and verbally abused by others as I grew up because I smelled of urine or wore dirty and outdated clothes daily.

I realize we did not have much financial stability as a family, given that mom's earnings were used for your addictions to alcohol and sex rather than providing for our family's needs. I understand you chose your addictions over my hygiene and having clean clothes.

Dad, you did unspeakable sexual things to me. These disgusting sexual things have vastly affected my marriage. How dare you pinch my breasts as you walked by and how you would proudly show me your sex toys and pornography. How dare you speak and make disgusting sexual comments and gestures and how you would drill in me the belief that if a woman is violated sexually in any way, it is always her fault.

I know you would have believed my husband's sex addiction was my fault; I am not allowing you that power anymore.

Your gross distortion of sexuality robbed me so much from enjoying the gift God wanted me to have. I hold you responsible for creating such distortions in my head.

I tried hard not to pass this on to my children, but somehow, your teachings found a way into the next generation of the family.

I hate that I missed out on such a gift God has given me because of what you have passed onto me. Because of you, I, unfortunately, had viewed sex as an evil activity between husband and wife.

You taught me not to feel because you did not know how to handle feelings. So many times, I was not allowed to express sadness, frustration, anger, fear, or joy because you stifled those feelings by physically abusing me and slapping my face so hard it would leave bruises.

God has guided me in progressing my emotions. Dad, you have robbed me of so much. Even writing this letter is difficult because I cannot adequately describe what I feel from the effects of your abusive actions.

You do not know how much I desired your love and approval. A sick part of me always wanted to please you in every way possible, and I now question what I may have allowed you to do to me just to earn your approval. This is sickening even having to consider.

As a result, in trying to earn your love and acceptance, I have hurt my siblings. Thank God they are not holding how I treated them against me today.

In your final days of life, you finally told me how much you loved me. What was I supposed to do with that? Dad, it was very confusing to hear the words "I love you" come from your mouth. How can someone say they love another when they continue to abuse them? That's a contradiction, Dad.

It was abusive how you treated me the way you did. No one in our family ever deserved to be treated like you treated us.

God has revealed that I have put your thoughts and opinions above his. I realize this is unhealthy and sinful, and I needed all along to have a reference for God and God alone.

God has put on my heart to continue to pursue healing through therapy, even though it is immensely challenging. Writing this letter to you helps to renounce your power over me. The beautiful part of this story is that God has and will continue to use my experiences for his glory, which I praise him for.

Dad, this is my official statement of proclaiming you do not have any more power or control over me, even from the grave. I will no longer allow myself to be controlled by your voice. No longer will your degrading verbal abuse have power over me. No longer will I seek your approval. My identity from this day forward will only come from my Heavenly Father, who will never fail me.

Claiming my true identity in Christ,
Melissa Roberts

In writing this letter, John helped me process everything buried deep down. I would not trade anything for the peace and joy I now feel after seven years of intensive therapy. It was worth every mile I traveled and every dollar spent and every agonizing moment I had to experience. I am now in a place of acceptance and peace.

Currently, I am a pastoral counselor working with abused women. In addition, I volunteer as a court-appointed special advocate (CASA). Being part of CASA allows me to advocate for abused or neglected children who end up in the court system. By having a voice for these children, I gave Little Melissa the ability to help her and others.

CHAPTER 9

My Life Today

The abundance of our lives is not
determined by how long we live, but how
well we live. Christ makes abundant life
possible if we choose to live it now.

—Barbra Brown Taylor

After the divorce was final, I found it difficult to mark "Divorced" on any papers I had to complete. I had to get used to it since it was never my life goal to have that label. Since then, however, I have developed a comfortable rhythm in life.

Through ongoing therapy, I strived to work on forgiveness. The process went much quicker after the divorce. For me, this was essential to be at peace with myself, others, and God.

It did not take long for me to enjoy living alone. I could do any activity without having to check in with anyone. I ate whatever I wanted whenever I wanted, although I attempted to eat as healthy as I could. Fortunately, I lived less than a quarter of a mile from an ice cream store, which became a source of palate pleasure. I had enjoyed the freedom to occasionally splurge by walking down to purchase a small dish of ice cream, usually if I felt I had a stressful day at school.

I also had control over what I wanted to watch on television. I did not watch shows that were gruesome and didn't immerse myself in the news. I attempted to keep my home atmosphere low-key and as stress-free as possible. Outside of my close friendships, my loyal in-house friend was Ali, who helped keep me from feeling lonely. Living alone gave me the control and freedom I needed—no more chaos and lies.

FINDING MY PASSION

Biking became a strong passion of mine, especially on the weekends and in the summer months when school was over. I strapped my bike on the back of my Ford Focus and headed to the nearest biking trail to bike twenty or thirty miles. I enjoyed riding as it became very relaxing and a form of stress release.

I often pushed myself out of my comfort zone to experience something new. In the past, I tended to stray away from new experiences for fear of inadequacy, failure, or inability. However, through therapy, I learned to ask myself what would be the worst thing possible when filled with fear.

I challenged myself to sign up for something out of my comfort zone: the "Michigander." The Michigander is a three-hundred-mile bike ride throughout Northern Michigan. The bike ride included riding near Lake Michigan and through towns such as Petoskey, Harbor Springs, Cheboygan, Charlevoix, and the famous Tunnel of Trees.

To prepare for this ride, I purchased a two-person tent that I learned to put up myself in the backyard of my home. I also purchased an inflatable air mattress to help me sleep on the ground comfortably. To get myself physically ready, I made it a goal to bike at least five times a week, thirty to forty miles per ride.

The excitement grew as it got closer to leaving. The question now became, Can I really do this alone? With determination in my veins, I knew I had to follow through with my plan.

The day of the ride finally arrived. The ride began in Cheboygan, a four-hour drive from my home. Having everything packed, I made my way up north. Upon my arrival, I pitched my tent on the high school grounds and settled in for the night as I wanted to get as much rest as possible for the early morning departure.

Early morning came, and I was instructed to pack all my belongings and take what I did not want to carry on my bike to the sag truck. The sag truck took everyone's gear to the next destination (layover). After loading my gear onto the truck, I ate breakfast.

The trip's biggest challenge was not putting up and taking down my tent every night but rather riding through the Tunnel of Trees. The route was narrow, curvy, and hilly, so riding was extremely challenging and dangerous if one was not careful.

There was this mishap where my bike chain slipped off, jamming my pedal. Of course, this happened as I attempted to shift, going uphill. As a result, it left me stranded on the narrow road with traffic coming from both directions.

Fortunately, a couple of younger men riding the Michigander stopped and assisted me so I could finish the ride for the day. Although it was a situation that left me feeling somewhat inadequate and vulnerable, I could put it all behind me as I continued on the ride.

After eight days of bicycling forty to sixty miles per day and seven nights of sleeping on the ground, I reached my goal of biking over three hundred miles that week.

There were no words to describe the ecstatic feeling of accomplishing my goal of completing the Michigander. It proved that I could achieve anything I set my mind to with determination. I felt so empowered and was ready to do another ride like this.

In the following year, I accomplished two other bike rides. The first bike ride was called a century ride, where I would have to bike one hundred miles in a day.

At that time, I was still a CASA volunteer. The director had to devise creative ways to raise monies for the program. I decided to have people sponsor me for each mile I rode in a day to help raise funds. I set the goal of raising $1,000. Unfortunately, I only biked up to fifty miles in one day, so I had to push myself to increase the miles I trained daily.

When the day arrived, I had about $800 pledged for my ride. Determined to reach my goal, I posted a live video on Facebook whenever I made stops on my route, describing the day's conditions, successes, and challenges I was having.

My biggest challenge was the constant twenty- to twenty-five-miles-per-hour winds pushing against me. By the end of my twelve-hour-per-day riding, I had completed over a hundred miles per day and raised $1,500 for the CASA program. *Not bad for a fifty-nine-year-old,* I told myself. Yes, in case you are wondering, was I exhausted and sore? Yes, very much so.

I knew going in that this was most likely a once-in-a-lifetime ride I would never do again. Looking back, I am so glad I did—it was a ride of a lifetime. Within three weeks, I was on my bike again, riding the "Pedal Across Lower Michigan," known as PALM.

This ride began in Holland with our back wheels in Lake Michigan and rode through the southern part of Michigan until we reached Luna Pier and stuck our front tires into Lake Erie.

The PALM ride appealed to me because we camped at the high school of the small town where I resided and because I was able to bike from Lake Michigan to Lake Erie. The ride went through many blueberry and grape orchards and other beautiful Michigan farm-lands. Pushing myself to go on these trips developed a love for adventure. I have never felt such freedom and true contentment as I felt during this time.

Even though much emotional healing had been accomplished, I continued to have therapy sessions with John periodically. We would talk about my accomplishments and the obstacles I was experiencing.

Male Relationship Challenges

One of the topics that I wanted to talk about with John was my challenge with opposite-sex relationships. Truthfully, I had little interest but knew I needed to address this with him. I became increasingly aware that I quickly put up my walls when someone was interested in me.

For one thing, I was content with living alone and enjoyed the freedom to do whatever I wanted, when I wanted, and how I wanted.

Secondly, I enjoyed the rhythm of my newly formed life, which I grew to like.

I knew I tended to become hurt and scared when any man came relationally close to me due to my experiences with my father and my ex-husband.

Having not dated before Barry, I never developed other close intimate relationships with men; I guess you could say I did not trust them. Going into the dating world conjured up feelings of fear and pain.

Having a gross distortion in sexuality because of my abusive history, I was unsure if I wanted to take a risk. Maybe some things are best left broken for life, which was how I protected myself from danger.

As you may recall, COVID-19 hit in March 2020, considerably challenging my thinking. In Michigan, when COVID-19 hit, most stores and restaurants immediately shut down, giving me no opportunity to get out. Interestingly, I thought I would make a great hermit since I did not want to be around other people.

When COVID hit, I could only walk with Ali or ride my bike—no going to the ice cream store or going out with friends.

Not long into the COVID pandemic, I received a phone call from my church informing me I had been exposed to COVID by someone I was ministering to. My first thought was, *Who?* Although the church did not tell me, I ended up having to be quarantined for two weeks for precautionary measures.

I was confined to my apartment for ten days. The challenge was that I had no one to turn to. Although a few church friends offered to drop grocery items on my porch, I had to live secluded.

It was out of boredom and curiosity that I started searching dating sites. Fearful of what I might find, I pushed myself. I remember conversations I had with John where he challenged my beliefs about men and dating; he knew I was allowing my fears to retake control. We talked, and I agreed the best site to test out was a Christian dating site.

After completing my profile, I immediately received a few responses, which left me feeling excited and curious all at the same time. However, I also needed to be cautious because I knew people were often deceived through internet dating sites.

Not soon after, I received messages from men asking "How many tattoos do you have?" "Do you have any body piercings, and if so, where?" and "What kind of car do you drive?" I even received messages from women who had an interest in me. *This is a new world of dating,* I thought, *especially on a Christian dating site.*

There were a few men I spent time messaging with. One man claimed he was an officer in the army and was stationed about two hours away. We reached a point in our messaging where we shared phone numbers to text. When we texted, he usually needed to know where I was and what I was doing. Thinking it was odd to be asked this, I contacted some friends to research him. Both were exceptionally talented at digging through Facebook and the internet to find information about people.

Both concluded that the "army man" in question was not an army man after all. I remembered earlier in our texting he had shared he might show up at my doorstep when I least expected it. Upon learning this, I immediately blocked his number.

It was not long before I began to communicate with another man. He claimed to be a CEO of a TV dish network in Wisconsin. Being naive, I did not see the warning signs, so I continued to correspond with him for a few weeks. Being somewhat intrigued, we agreed to use FaceTime to meet. It turned into a disaster because his internet connection was weak. He also had a heavy foreign accent.

This time I became wiser and concluded that he most likely lived in another country and portrayed himself as someone other than who he was. After that, I told myself I was done going to dating websites to look for a decent guy. Besides, my ten days of quarantine were long over, so I could at least get out of the house.

As a result, I immediately removed my profile and vowed never again to use an online dating website. I did my best to stay busy while everything was shut down by taking walks in the local park and riding my bike. I also learned to connect via Zoom with several Bible study groups I was involved with. Even though it was not the same, it did help me to stay connected with others.

Throughout the pandemic, I had to isolate myself just like everyone else. However, six months later, I contracted COVID and had to quarantine. After I recovered from the initial effects of COVID (high fever, coughing, loss of taste and smell, and extreme tiredness), loneliness quickly crept in. Again, gracious friends would drop much-needed items on my porch, but I missed the personal interaction.

After the worst of COVID had passed, I once again became curious and searched online for a safer online dating service.

I did not search with dating in mind; instead, I wanted someone for companionship, someone I could be friends with. With all the therapy I had been through, I would at least be comfortable with male friendship.

Being wiser now, I did not seek a Christian dating site because I felt there would be more predators preying on the word *Christian*. My new, wiser profile stated I was a conservative Christian who only desired others who shared the same values as I did.

My new profile included a picture of me in my biking attire. I was searching for two qualities in a male friend: (1) he would have to prove he was a strong Christian, and (2) he would have a passion for bike riding. He would have to live locally, no more than an hour away, as I believed connecting with anyone long distance would be too complicated.

A few days later, I received a message from Charles stating he was a firm Christian believer and loved bike riding. He inquired about what bike trips I had taken. My thought was, so far, so good; he wanted to know more about my bike trips. *No harm in that,* I thought.

Charles told me he typically liked to bike over one thousand miles yearly, which, I must say, impressed me. I learned he lived only twenty-five miles from me based on the respective zip codes we exchanged.

In time, I felt he met every criterion I had listed for a male friend. But I still had one more task I needed to accomplish before I allowed this to go any further. After we exchanged our last names,

I had my friend do an internet search on him to determine if everything lined up with his claims.

After a few days, my friend told me everything he said lined up. We also learned that his son-in-law was a pastor of a large church. As it turned out, some of his adult children were friends with some young adults I knew at my church.

Amazingly, everything she showed me on Facebook was very encouraging. I felt this might have potential, but I still needed to be cautious, for I did not want to be hurt again.

Within a week, we exchanged phone numbers and began texting daily. Within a few weeks, we decided to FaceTime and communicated more personally. Part of me was frightened because I was waiting for the shoe to drop, but I was also encouraged by what seemed very promising.

As we FaceTimed together, I was impressed with this man. Charles was sixty-seven and had undergone heart and liver transplants about five years prior. He told me of his struggles and joys of going through all that, which was impressive. He told me it was probably one of the highlights of his life because he saw God's hand all over his healing.

Charles shared that he had lost his wife of forty-three years to cancer three years after his transplants. My heart began to melt upon learning his story, and I sensed a deep genuineness within him. Additionally, I was impressed that he was easy to talk to and had a great sense of humor.

Since FaceTiming went well, we both decided that we needed to go to the next step, which was to meet up in person. The only problem was that every establishment was shut down due to COVID.

As it turned out, my church had reopened for live, in-person service, so we discussed meeting at my church. However, Charles expressed that he wanted to wait another couple of weeks after my recovery from COVID since he was immunosuppressed due to his transplants. Of course, I had no issues agreeing with his request.

The weekend of our meeting at my church was quickly approaching. After some thought, I decided I wanted to meet with Charles before he came to my church. I wanted to know beforehand the person to whom I was introducing my friends. Since Charles and I enjoyed hiking, I decided to ask if we could meet at a hiking path near his home the day before we met at church. He agreed.

When Saturday morning came, I became anxious. What did I think when I suggested meeting for the first time in a wooded area? He could easily drag me off the beaten path and do something terrible. As my mind raced, I thought he might be an axe murderer, and I would somehow disappear, never to be seen again. What was I thinking?

I did not want to cancel the date, so I created safeguards to protect myself. First, I talked to some of my friends, letting them know where and when I would be there. One friend offered to be on text alert, stating that if I needed anything, to text her, and she would immediately get in her car and come to my assistance. The other safeguard I utilized was having some pepper spray hidden underneath my coat jacket sleeve in case I needed it.

When I arrived, Charles was waiting in his car. Before leaving my vehicle, I texted my friend to ask for a quick prayer for safety. After our prayer, I exited my car and took a deep breath, praying that I had not made a mistake.

Charles stood six feet, three inches tall. He presented himself as a gentle giant compared to my five-foot-three body. To my surprise, he pulled out a giant walking stick as he exited his silver van, slightly increasing my anxiety. He greeted me with a robust smile that shined like a bright, sunny day. Something about him lessened my fears and insecurities, although I still had my pepper spray secretly hidden, just in case.

We hiked and talked for about four miles before returning to our cars. I had never met a man who was so easy to talk to. Listening intently to him, I learned he was a gifted storyteller.

He told me more about his family, details of his transplant, and his passion for bike riding. I also learned he was a man of God who enjoyed life despite his health issues and the loss of his wife.

I shared some of my past childhood and marriage abuse and struggles. As I talked, I noted he was a great listener and empathized with what I shared. This was indeed a new experience.

Charles offered for me to follow him in my car to his home, which was nearby, for Chinese food from a nearby restaurant and perhaps a few games of cards. I agreed to follow him. However, before leaving the parking lot, I texted my friend, letting her know I was okay and going to his house for food and a game of cards or two. I assured her that I felt safe. I remember telling her I still had my pepper spray strapped to my arm if anything occurred.

The evening went very well. Charles and I continued to share and laugh together, and I especially enjoyed listening to his humorous stories.

Although I lost three hands of cribbage, I did not mind as I felt I was gaining a new friend. I went home feeling lighthearted and was glad we took the time to meet each other before our scheduled church plans.

We met up again the next day at my church. I was extremely comfortable introducing him to my friends. They were also impressed, and they laughed and joked with us.

It was such a relief that my friends approved. Despite my history of trauma, I was becoming excited about the future. I never expected to enjoy the companionship of a male friend. As I reflect, it was worth all my hard work in therapy with John.

Things Are Warming Up

Over the next few months, Charles and I met for church, hikes, and bike rides. Within a few months, I realized I was falling in love, which I never expected. But I was the one who fell in love first. He explained that it was only two years since his wife had passed, and he did not know if he was ready. A month later, on Valentine's Day evening, after we attended a banquet at my church, he surprised me by telling me he was in love with me.

In early October 2021, Charles and I married in the church where his son-in-law pastored. Both his son-in-law and my pastor officiated the ceremony. My only apprehension was how I would respond when we became sexually intimate.

Over months of dating, Charles did not put any pressure on me regarding holding hands, hugging, or kissing. He had learned most of my history and never took advantage of me or our situation.

Charles was a true gentleman and even asked if he could open my car door. This warmed my heart to no end. We discussed our expectations of sexual intimacy because we both had experienced issues in our prior marriages. I talked to John and God about our sexual concerns and felt aligned in trusting God in the healing process.

We have been married for sixteen months now as I write this. Living life is so much fun. Although there are challenges and not everything is rainbows and unicorns, I am living the dream.

Several adjustments included moving to a new city, blending our families, and readjusting my preferred ways of doing things to *our* way of doing things.

Charles and I have been on a nonstop adventure since we married. We rode over 1,500 miles, hiked miles of trails, and kayaked streams and lakes. Even sex has been a rewarding adventure. I thoroughly love being married to Charles.

Looking back along my journey, I remember God's spirit telling me I would eventually have a healthy marriage. Admittedly, I thought it would be a marriage with Barry. However, God had other plans. I still pray for Barry that he, too, will find healing and life with another. God is so good!

SECTION III

Recovery—Stages of Grief and Loss

JOHN STERNFELS,
LPC, NCC, CSAT, CMAT, CCPS, C-SASI

What to Expect

If you don't feel your best today, allow
yourself that space. This is hard, and you
don't have to process this all at once.

—Unknown

Grief is universal and is a highly individualized experience. It is a complex and multifaceted experience involving various emotions, thoughts, and behaviors, and there is no right or wrong way to grieve, as everyone experiences grief differently. How a person grieves depends on many factors, including their personality, coping style, life experience, faith, and the loss that was significant to them.

There seems to be a familiar pattern when a person experiences grief or loss, whether from losing a loved one or being betrayed by an unfaithful spouse in what was considered to be a safe and secure relationship. Grief can also be the result of being emotionally or sexually abused. Grief and loss can be overwhelming, and getting stuck in pain can be easy.

The six stages of grief and loss are not neat or necessarily linear and do not follow timelines. Out of the blue, you may cry, become angry, withdraw, or feel empty, and none of these emotional states are unusual or wrong. It is important to remember that everyone grieves differently, but there are some commonalities in the stages and the order of feelings experienced during grief and loss.[3]

Getting stuck in grief and loss can also include withdrawal periods or distancing oneself from healthy relationships. It can even result in developing food, drug, or alcohol addictions. The pain can increase any unresolved anger and cause hourly or daily moodiness. If a person remains stuck in any stage of grief and loss, they can often become consumed by it, resulting in a loss of life focus, purpose, and direction.

---

[3] "The Stages of Grief: How to Understand Your Feelings," Healthline, https://www.healthline.com/health/stages-of-grief.

In 1969, a Swiss-American psychiatrist named Elisabeth Kübler-Ross wrote in her book *On Death and Dying* that grief could be divided into five stages. Her observations came from years of working with terminally ill individuals.[4]

Dr. Kübler-Ross theorized that grief, known as the Kübler-Ross model, had five stages: denial, anger, bargaining, depression, and acceptance.[5] While it was initially devised for people who were ill, these stages of grief have been adapted for other experiences with loss as well.[6]

Although these five stages of grief may be the most widely known, they are far from the only popular stages theorized today. Admittedly, several others exist; however, we will utilize a six-stage model. In working with trauma, grief, and loss for over a decade, we found using a six-stage model provides a more realistic model of understanding.

Grief and loss can be extremely overwhelming and powerful. The six general stages of grief are as follows:

First stage: Shock
Second stage: Denial
Third stage: Anger
Fourth stage: Bargaining
Fifth stage: Sadness/Depression
Sixth stage: Acceptance

Grief has a way of grabbing you without warning and doesn't let go. Grief can weaken the immune system, leaving us prone to colds and other illnesses. Grief also affects our appetite and sleep patterns and increases susceptibilities to headaches, stomachaches, and body aches. Other bodily effects include joint pain, inflammation, not to mention digestive difficulties and other problems.

---

4 "Stages of Grief."
5 "Stages of Grief."
6 "Stages of Grief."

Other physical and emotional symptoms include sadness, lack of energy or fatigue, lack of motivation, and periods of hopelessness and despair. Also included are memory lapses, distraction, anger, rage, confusion, and irritability. Excessive sleeping or overworking or bouts of extreme activity are all designed to help numb the pain.

Spiritual symptoms can include feelings of being deeply connected to God or having extreme anger and outrage at God. Many people question or blame God in times of grief due to the unrealistic expectation that he should protect them from life's adversities.

Regardless of the symptoms, it takes time to heal from grief and loss, which are natural human processes that all of us must experience at one time or another. No matter how we may want to stop the hurt, we need to accept the natural grieving process.

Inevitably, the grieving process requires time. It is essential to know not to rush the process and that healing happens gradually; it cannot be forced or hurried, and there is no "normal" timetable for grieving. While some people may start to feel better in weeks or months, for others, the grieving process is measured in years. Whatever your grief experience, it is essential to be patient with yourself and allow the process to unfold naturally.[7]

---

[7] "Coping with Grief and Loss," HelpGuide, https://www.helpguide.org/articles/grief/coping-with-grief-and-loss.htm.

CHAPTER 10

First Stage—Shock

There is no time stamp on trauma. There isn't
a formula that you can insert yourself into to
get from horror to healed. Be patient. Take
up space. Let your journey be the balm.

—Dawn Serra

Whatever type of grief and loss you may be experiencing, there is no right or wrong way to grieve. We hope you will find healthy ways to cope and regain control of your life by reading and understanding the six phases of grief and loss.

Chances are, you are reading this book due to having experienced some degree of grief and loss resulting in *emotional shock*. Emotional shock can hit hard; experiencing emotional shock is how our mind and body react to the normal process of experiencing something terrible. Getting through the pain or fear and feeling safe again can take time when bad things happen.

There may be no outward visible signs of physical injury for many, but it can take an overwhelming emotional toll. It is common for people who experience trauma or difficulty to have an initial emotional reaction known as *shock*.

It is known that emotional and psychological trauma result from extraordinary stressful events that shatter one's sense of security, making one feel confused and helpless and further adding pain, numbness, disconnectedness, and an inability to trust oneself or others.

This shock stage is a reaction that causes a rush of overwhelming emotions that a person is not ready to understand or respond to, which causes their body to go into a state of shock. Dr. Daramus, a licensed clinical psychologist, states it this way, "Emotional shock is often part of the fight-or-flight response, a normal but painful way our brain reacts to something it sees as a threat to our well-being."[8]

When our brain cannot process a situation, it freezes to protect our mind and body. We may feel numb, cry, or rage. Other times, we may just sit there, emotionally unable to move. We may tend to dissociate and think that nothing around us is real or that it is happening to someone else.

Symptoms of emotional shock can include the following:[9]

- numbness
- disassociation
- panic
- breathlessness
- headache
- nausea
- dizziness
- light-headedness
- muscle tension
- increased heart rate
- tightness in the throat or chest
- inability to speak or move
- difficulty rationalizing, thinking, or planning
- loss of interest in the surroundings
- inability to express emotion

---

[8] "Emotional Shock: Definition, Symptoms, Causes, and Treatment," https://www.verywellmind.com/emotional-shock-definition-symptoms-causes-and-treatment-5214434.

[9] "Emotional Shock."

It is important to note that even though two people may face the same experience, they may have completely different emotional reactions. No one should judge what is right to feel and what is not—everyone is different!

Experiencing emotional shock may vary from person to person. This, of course, depends upon the severity and circumstance of the situation. It may linger for a few minutes or persist longer (e.g., hours, days, or months). If it lasts longer, this may lead to what is known as acute distress disorder (ASD) or post-traumatic stress disorder (PTSD).

Although it is not within the scope of this book to go into great depth regarding these two mental health diagnoses, we will briefly discuss each below.

According to the US Department of Veterans Affairs,[10] *PTSD: National Center for PTSD* states that acute stress disorder is "a mental health problem that can occur in the first month after a traumatic event. The symptoms of ASD are like PTSD symptoms, but you must have them for longer than one month to have PTSD."

Dr. Elizabeth Scott, wellness coach, author, and educator, writes, "During an acute stress response, the autonomic nervous system is activated and the body experiences increased levels of cortisol, adrenaline and other hormones that produce an increased heart rate, quickened breathing rate, and higher blood pressure."[11]

The Mayo Clinic states, "Post-traumatic stress disorder [PTSD] is a mental health condition that is triggered by a terrifying event—either experiencing it or witnessing it. Symptoms may include flashbacks, nightmares, severe anxiety, and uncontrollable thoughts about the event."[12]

Post-traumatic stress disorder symptoms may start within one month of a traumatic event, but sometimes "symptoms may not

[10] "United States: Korean War Veterans 'Ambassador for Peace' Medal Ceremony Scheduled," MENA Report (Albawaba [London] Ltd., Nov. 2018).
[11] "Emotional Shock."
[12] "Post-Traumatic Stress Disorder [PTSD]—Symptoms and Causes," https://www.mayoclinic.org/diseases-conditions/post-traumatic-stress-disorder/symptoms-causes/syc-20355967.

appear until years after. These symptoms cause significant problems in social or work situations resulting in interpersonal challenges that can interfere with your ability to perform typical daily tasks."[13]

PTSD symptoms are generally grouped into four types: intrusive memories, avoidance, negative changes in thinking and mood, and changes in physical and emotional reactions. Symptoms can vary over time or vary from person to person.[14]

To further help explain the four group types, the Mayo Clinic reports the following:

Symptoms of intrusive memories:[15]

- recurrent, unwanted distressing memories of the traumatic event
- reliving the traumatic event as if it were happening again (flashbacks)
- upsetting dreams or nightmares about the traumatic event
- severe emotional distress or physical reactions to something that reminds you of the traumatic event

Symptoms of avoidance:[16]

- trying to avoid thinking or talking about the traumatic event
- avoiding places, activities, or people that remind you of the traumatic event

---

[13] "PTSD—Symptoms and Causes."

[14] "PTSD—Symptoms and Causes."

[15] "Post-Traumatic Stress Disorder [PTSD]—Comforts of Home Counseling," https://www.comfortsofhomecounseling.com/counseling-therapy-services/individual-therapy/post-traumatic-stress-disorder/.

[16] "PTSD—Comforts of Home Counseling."

Symptoms of negative changes in thinking and mood:[17]

- negative thoughts about yourself, other people, or the world
- hopelessness about the future
- memory problems, including not remembering important aspects of the traumatic event
- difficulty maintaining close relationships
- feeling detached from family and friends
- lack of interest in activities you once enjoyed
- difficulty experiencing positive emotions
- feeling emotionally numb

Examples of symptoms in physical and emotional reactions:[18]

- being easily startled or frightened
- always being on guard for danger
- self-destructive behavior, such as drinking too much or driving too fast
- trouble sleeping
- trouble concentrating
- irritability, angry outbursts, or aggressive behavior
- overwhelming guilt or shame

Experiencing a traumatic event(s) may cause temporary difficulty adjusting and coping. However, it usually gets better with time and healthy self-care. If the symptoms worsen, last for months or even years, and interfere with your day-to-day functioning, it is best to get evaluated for PTSD.[19]

When we experience a traumatic event, our bodies will secrete a flood of stress hormones, which can cause us to experience three basic reactions. The three responses are *fight*, *flight*, and *freeze* (immobility).

---

[17] "PTSD—Comforts of Home Counseling."
[18] "Can PTSD Cause Disorientation?" StudyBuff, https://studybuff.com/can-ptsd-cause-disorientation/.
[19] "PTSD—Symptoms and Causes."

Fight. A fight trauma reaction results from believing one can maintain power and/or control over the apparent threat. This can be best seen when someone yells, fights, screams, is physically aggressive, or throws things.

The fight trauma response involves a release of hormones (primarily cortisol and adrenaline) in the body that triggers a reaction to stay and ward off or "fight" the apparent threat. The sympathetic nervous system is responsible for the reactions that occur within the body during this stress response.[20]

Flight. The flight response is when we don't understand the situation entirely. The flight trauma response involves a release of stress hormones that signal us to flee from danger or threat. Instead of staying in a dangerous situation, this response causes us to literally or metaphorically run.

The flight trauma response involves the release of adrenaline and noradrenaline. These are our emergency hormones, which are rapidly released in reaction to stress of any kind and during emergency situations. These hormones stimulate alertness, pupil dilation, perspiration, and other bodily functions.

Freeze. When we are in a state of shock, we may tend to freeze in disbelief. Although freezing serves adaptive purposes, it can harm our mental health. We can feel guilt, shame, and self-directed anger if we have not protected ourselves. It is important to remember that freezing is an unconscious defense mechanism and offers the best chance of survival at the moment.

While in shock, our minds may go blank, leaving us struggling to defend ourselves, and it is only when the perceived threat has passed that we think of things we could have said or done differently. When we experience shock, we may react exaggeratedly to when we are surprised. We open our eyes wide to process the situation and open our mouths, ready to scream or take in air to breathe and run for the hills. Freezing can give us time to decide if we are in personal danger or not.

---

[20] "Sympathetic Nervous System—an Overview," ScienceDirect Topics, https://www.sciencedirect.com/topics/neuroscience/sympathetic-nervous-system.

Whether in a fight, flight, or freeze state, Psychiatrist Caroline Fisher breaks it down this way: "During the response, all bodily systems are working to keep us alive in what we've perceived as a dangerous situation."[21]

21 "What Happens during Fight-or-Flight Response," Cleveland Clinic, https://health.clevelandclinic.org/what-happens-to-your-body-during-the-fight-or-flight-response/.

CHAPTER 11

Second Stage—Denial

The attempt to escape from pain
is what creates more pain.

—Gabor Maté

The second stage in grief and loss is *denial*. Denial is the refusal to believe or accept something as being true. It is a coping response designed to provide self-protection from having to deal with anxiety and reality. The belief is that if a person tells themselves "No, that's not true," "It's not that bad," or "It really didn't happen," they don't have to deal with the objective truth. Even if the person knows it has happened, it is a way to avoid dealing with the reality of the situation or circumstance.

Anyone can experience denial, which arises from events or circumstances that make us feel that our well-being and/or control are being challenged or threatened. However, those who suffer from trauma are more susceptible to denial due to the invasive nature of the trauma.

Although it is quite natural to reject the idea that something did happen, it makes it no less painful when having to confront the truth. In time, a person may isolate themselves to avoid reminders of the truth. When others, such as friends or family, wish to provide comfort, it may cause further complications while the person still faces grief and loss.

Psychology identifies denial as the primary defense mechanism most of us use to cope with highly stressful situations. It often involves blocking external events from conscious awareness.

Essentially, if a situation is too much for someone, they may refuse to experience it. That does not make the situation's facts or reality disappear, but it allows the person to pretend it is not real, reducing its impact on them. At least one may perceive that the impact is reduced.[22]

Often, people develop unconscious defense mechanisms to address contradictions in their lives. In managing the various demands of their careers, relationships, and personal lives, it can be easy for someone to feel threatened or overwhelmed, which is a precursor to anxiety. As a result, the human body and brain can create defense mechanisms like denial to help people cope with uncomfortable feelings like anxiety and guilt.[23]

While denial may reduce someone's anxiety in the short term, eventually, the reality of the circumstances will show back up, and it may be more challenging to manage the issue at that point.[24]

As mentioned, denial is a normal reaction to stressful situations, as denial gives the mind time to unconsciously take in shocking or distressful information without sending people into shock. However, it can be unhealthy when a person stays in denial, and if denial persists, it can prevent a person from taking action to deal with their issue.

Sometimes, denial is evident through bits of anger and extreme emotion. On the other hand, it can also be far more subtle, to the point where the person in denial honestly does not realize it. Although it is a normal reaction to circumstances out of a person's control, denial can be a significant obstacle to one's healing.

Anxiety, fear, and insecurity can all bring about denial. As a natural human instinct, people try to protect their emotional security. Sometimes, when an event threatens people or scares them, these

---

[22] "What Is Denial Psychology and How to Address It," BetterHelp, https://www.betterhelp.com/advice/general/what-is-denial-psychology-how-to-address-it/.

[23] "What Is Denial Psychology."

[24] "What Is Denial Psychology."

emotions can be shoved to the side as a coping mechanism.[25] Due to a natural protection mechanism, people can fall into denial without even realizing it.

It can be difficult for a person in this stage to recognize they need help due to being in denial.

The following are symptoms and signs a person is in denial:

- avoidance of talking about this subject
- procrastinating
- minimizing by saying "It's no big deal," "I'm fine," or "It's fine"
- projecting onto others what you do not want to see in yourself
- forgetting
- keeping busy
- comparing one's behavior, trying to prove there isn't a problem
- rationalizing one's behaviors
- ignoring the concern and advice from family and friends

In summary, there may be times we do not want to accept the truth of a situation for various reasons. However, it is important to know that denial is usually not the best way to resolve something adversely affecting you. Denying an issue can create additional challenges in your life. It is important to know that there are ways to move from denial to acceptance at a pace that is right for you.[26]

[25] "What Is Psychological Denial?" Camomi Enoteca, https://www.camomienoteca.com/research-paper-help/what-is-psychological-denial/.
[26] "What Is Denial Psychology."

CHAPTER 12

Third Stage—Anger

You are stronger than you think. You
have gotten through every bad day in
your life, and you are undefeated.

—Unknown

The third stage in grief and loss is *anger*. Although it is referred to as
the third stage, we feel it is better to think of anger as a state rather
than a stage. A stage is often seen as a phase leading to another or,
ultimately, the end result. It would be better to see anger as a *state*
during the grieving and loss process where the circumstances or conditions of life are such that anger might easily be the response.[27] It
is important to remember that these stages can happen in any order,
for varying durations, and in combination, not just one at a time in
the exact order.[28]

Once the individual has stopped denying the loss, the reality of
the situation begins to set in, bringing additional confusion, anger,
frustration, and pain. The mind and body begin to process that pain
and express it as anger. The anger may be aimed at an inanimate

---

[27] https://www.econdolence.com/learning-center/grief-and-coping/the-stages-of-
grief/second-stage-of-grief-anger/.

[28] "3 Steps to Work through the Anger Stage of Grief," Thriveworks, https://
thriveworks.com/blog/grief-becomes-anger-work-through-grieving-process/.

object, like pounding their fists on the table, throwing things on the floor, or hitting the wall out of anger and frustration.[29]

Other times, it is aimed at people, whether strangers, friends, or family members. Often, the anger is aimed at the perpetrator or the loved one who betrayed them. As previously mentioned, the stages are not necessarily linear, leaving this state of anger or rage a cyclical process. They may feel guilty for being angry, leading to even more forms of anger.

It is natural to feel angry due to the loss of something that was important to you, and the first step is to understand where your anger comes from. Kriss Kevorkian, PhD, an internationally known expert in grief, states, "When anger is involved, it's important to look at it and find out if you're angry about the situation, the person [who offended you], or perhaps even God." Kevorkian continues by stating, "The best tip is to discuss this with a grief counselor who can help the person with his/her grieving process and find ways for that individual to cope with the loss he/she has had."[30]

Kevorkian explains that anger may result from the person having to deal with life on their own since a loved one has "abused, abandoned, or betrayed them." It is easy to see how feelings of sadness, fear, and pain can easily manifest as anger.[31]

Melissa Hudson, a psychotherapist specializing in marriage and family therapy (LMFT), explains how confronting the unpleasant feelings of sadness, fear, and pain can help a person better understand their anger and ultimately help them heal from the loss they must face.

The anger stage (state) of grief can feel overwhelming and confusing. You may ask yourself, "Why am I so angry?" Feeling confused, you ask yourself, "Is this a good thing?" It is crucial to know that anger is a secondary emotion; underneath it is a primary emotion,

---

[29] https://www.econdolence.com/learning-center/grief-and-coping/the-stages-of-grief/second-stage-of-grief-anger/.

[30] "Anger Stage of Grief."

[31] "An Age of Uncertainty: Mental Health in Young People," *The Lancet*, https://www.thelancet.com/journals/lancet/article/PIIS0140-6736(22)01572-0/fulltext.

often sadness or fear. It is often helpful to slow yourself down and ask "What is my fear?" or "What is the root of my sadness?" These questions and, more importantly, the answers will highlight what concerns you are still working with regarding your grief and loss.[32]

Hudson writes,

> When we suppress feelings, stuff them, or ignore them, they don't go away—they are just unresolved. Unfortunately, there is no going around and skipping hard feelings, and there is only going through it to reach acceptance. And when we have unresolved feelings, they often come up unexpectedly. If you kick feelings under the rug, I assure you: You will continue to trip over them. So face it, name it, feel it, and you will have it behind you sooner than later.[33]

The following are symptoms and signs a person is in a stage of anger:

- angry at oneself for experiencing or allowing the trauma or abuse to happen
- angry at the situation that left a person feeling powerless
- anger toward God for allowing the situation to happen
- angry at others who do not understand
- angry at others for being happy

---

[32] "Anger Stage of Grief."
[33] "Anger Stage of Grief."

CHAPTER 13

Fourth Stage—Bargaining

Resilience is accepting your new reality, even if
it's less good than the one you had before. You
can fight it, you can do nothing but scream
about what you've lost, or you can accept that
and try to put together something that's good.

—Elizabeth Edwards

The fourth stage in grief and loss is *bargaining*. The American
Psychological Association (APA) defines bargaining as a stage in
which a person may try to negotiate with themselves or with a higher
power (God) to try to undo the loss.

During this stage of grief and loss, the person may feel vulnerable and helpless. In those moments of intense emotions, it is not
uncommon to look for ways to regain control or to want to feel like
you can affect the outcome of an event. In the bargaining stage of
grief, you may create a lot of *what-if* and *if-only* statements.[34]

It is also not uncommon for faith-based individuals to try to
make a deal or a promise to God or a higher power in return for healing or relief from the grief and pain they are experiencing. Bargaining

---

[34] "The Stages of Grief: How to Understand Your Feelings," Healthline, https://www.healthline.com/health/stages-of-grief.

is a line of defense against the emotions of grief and helps the person postpone the sadness, confusion, or hurt.[35]

Therapist E. Krull, a licensed mental health professional (LMHP), writes, "Bargaining is the mind's way of pushing off reality. If the person allows the loss to sink in, they admit it is real and final. The mind is stubborn, so it scrambles and fights off the truth instead." Krull further states, "As you bargain with yourself or the universe, you may try to explain the loss or resolve your emotional pain in several ways."[36]

- You offer to be a better person, volunteer your time somewhere, or donate money if your emotional pain is taken away.
- You beat yourself up with guilt, saying that your loss would not have happened if you had done this or that.
- You bargain with a higher power or the universe, hoping for healing or a miracle to bring back what you lost.[37]

Even though grieving is a personal and unique journey for everyone, people typically feel similar emotions during the bargaining stage. Individuals may fervently want to delay or subdue the pain, undo the past, or take control of the situation. For instance, a person may fall into depression from grief, experience guilt from the thought that they could have prevented the loss or fatal event, or experience and express different types of anger.

Examples of feelings during the bargaining stage:

- anguish
- shame and guilt
- self-loathing
- anger

---

[35] "Stages of Grief."
[36] "What Happens during the Bargaining Stage of Grief?" Cake Blog, https://www.joincake.com/blog/bargaining-stage-of-grief/.
[37] "Bargaining Stage of Grief."

- resentment
- feeling betrayed by God (higher power)
- desperation for the pain to go away
- insecurity

Examples of when a person may be in the bargaining stage:

- If only I had stopped it, it would not have happened.
- I should have yelled for help.
- If only I were more attentive to him/her.
- I should have known better.
- Maybe if I were more sexual, then they would not have acted out.
- Perhaps if I were not a problem child, it would not have happened.
- If only _____.

CHAPTER 14

Fifth Stage—Sadness/Depression

You can't truly heal from a loss until you
allow yourself to really feel the loss.
—Mandy Hale

The fifth stage in grief and loss is *sadness/depression*. In this stage, empty feelings present themselves, and grief enters the person's life much more profoundly than ever imagined. This stage can feel as though it will last forever. It is important to understand that this sadness/depression is not a sign of mental illness and is the appropriate response to a significant loss.[38]

Floods of emotions that usually accompany the grieving process can lead to sadness/depression, as the grief and loss may seem too much to bear. Again, it is normal to experience temporary emotional reactions due to a loss or disappointment, which generally passes in a few days. Grief, however, is less an emotional reaction to something and more an actual personification of loss. It is the experience of being changed by the loss.

Sadness/depression is when the significant loss becomes more real, which can profoundly impact a person's life. Many may naturally want to withdraw from life or wonder if life is even worth living.

---

[38] "The 6 Stages of Grieving: How to Re-engage in Life after a Crushing Loss," Presence, https://presencelearning.com/insights/6-stages-of-grieving/.

When we grieve, we embody the sense of loss. We do not feel the grief; we are the grief. We encompass all that grief is. There is also a physical experience of suffering—wanting to isolate and draw into ourselves. Cognitively, there is also a sense of disorganization and a lack of focus. It is intertwined with cognitions, feelings, and bodily sensations.[39]

It's important to remember when a person confronts a debilitating loss, depression is not a symptom of a mental health condition. Instead, it is a natural and appropriate response to grief. Depression is the sensation of the heartbreak and emptiness we feel when navigating reality and realizing that the person or situation has changed in a way we do not want or had wished for. Again, in this stage, the grieving person may withdraw from life, feel numb, live in a fog, and not want to get out of bed in the morning to confront life. It is too overwhelming.[40]

It can be very challenging to gather the strength to face another day in the world. There is no interest in being around others or talking to anyone—only feelings of helplessness and hopelessness. Suicidal thoughts may even accompany depression. A person may wonder, *What's the point of going on?*[41]

> It's important to remember when a person confronts a debilitating loss, depression is not a symptom of a mental health condition.

Feeling sad or depressed is part of the human condition. But it is important to know what makes it different so you can figure out when you or someone you care about needs more support.[42]

---

39 "6 Stages of Grieving."
40 "6 Stages of Grieving."
41 "6 Stages of Grieving."
42 "What's the Difference between Sadness and Depression?" JED, https://jed-foundation.org/resource/whats-the-difference-between-sadness-and-depression/.

When a person experiences depression, sadness and anger may linger and not leave. It is as if a permanent, dark black cloud or fog is all around them.

Events or circumstances contributing to depression can be many, but regardless of the cause, it may not be easy to move through on your own.

You may also feel sad, guilty, hopeless, or numb with or without an apparent reason. Those feelings can linger for weeks or even months.[43]

What Depression Can Look Like

The biggest thing differentiating depression from sadness is how long it lasts and how much it affects your life. To be diagnosed with major depressive disorder, which is the clinical term, you need to have symptoms of depression for more than two weeks.

Depression can cause mild symptoms you can manage by making some changes on your own, as well as more severe symptoms that need medical attention, such as suicidal thoughts.[44]

We typically think of depression as feeling sad or down for an extended period, but there are lots of other symptoms of depression that we should be aware of, including the following:[45]

- Frequently or constantly feeling sad, empty, hopeless, frustrated, irritable, or pessimistic.
- Unintentional changes in appetite, such as eating too little or too much.
- Changes in sleeping patterns, such as being unable to sleep (insomnia) or sleeping too much (hypersomnia).
- Feeling tired or low on energy.

---

[43] "Difference between Sadness and Depression."
[44] "Difference between Sadness and Depression."
[45] "Difference between Sadness and Depression."

- Being less interested in activities you usually like or enjoying them less than you used to.
- Having trouble concentrating or remembering things.
- Feeling guilty, worthless, or like you are not enough.
- Feeling overwhelmed and unable to tackle new challenges or seek help.
- Not taking care of yourself, including skipping showers, not brushing your teeth, or avoiding other personal-hygiene tasks.
- Using alcohol or drugs to deal with difficult feelings or situations.
- Preferring not to socialize with family and friends.
- Frequently having thoughts of death or suicide. Suicidal thoughts can range from "I wish I wasn't around" or "I wish I were dead" to planning how to end your life.

Signs of depression can look different depending on your age, gender, and cultural background. They may include the following:[46]

- Crying spells or angry outbursts
- Moving or talking more slowly than usual
- Pacing, fidgeting, or being unable to sit still
- Falling behind on homework, chores, or other obligations
- Not enjoying things like you used to
- Fighting with family or friends
- Avoiding social interactions, such as not answering texts or skipping class or social events
- Comments expressing guilt, including, "I don't deserve to be with other people" or "I'm bringing you down"
- Changes in sleep, such as staying up later, waking up earlier, struggling to get up, or napping more often
- Having a hard time making decisions, answering questions, or thinking clearly

---

[46] "Difference between Sadness and Depression."

- Using alcohol or drugs to cope with difficult feelings or circumstances
- Self-harm

Sometimes depression symptoms appear in your body as physical feelings, such as frequent unexplained headaches, stomachaches, or back pain. Other times, medical issues look like or overlap with—or worsen—symptoms of depression. Chronic pain, migraines, and thyroid disorders can feel like—or cause—depressive symptoms.[47]

Kübler-Ross and Kessler say that depression is one of the many *necessary steps* in the healing process.[48]

- As tough as it is, depression can be dealt with paradoxically.
- See it as a visitor, perhaps an unwelcome one, but one who is visiting whether you like it or not.
- Make a place for your guest by allowing your depression to pull up a chair with you in front of the fire and sit with it without looking for a way to escape.
- Allow the sadness and emptiness to cleanse you and help you explore your loss.
- When you allow yourself to experience depression, it will leave as soon as it has served its purpose in your loss.
- As you grow stronger, it may return occasionally, but that is how grief works.

Help for Dealing with Depression[49]

Give yourself permission to feel your feelings. Don't let anyone tell you how you should feel or "You should get over it" or "Move on."

Don't try to suppress your grief. You must acknowledge your pain to heal. Avoiding your grief on a long-term basis can lead to com-

---

[47] "Difference between Sadness and Depression."

[48] "5 Stages of Grief and How to Survive Them," Love Lives On, https://www.loveliveson.com/5-stages-of-grief/.

[49] "5 Stages of Grief."

plications such as clinical depression, anxiety, substance abuse, and other health problems.

Express your feelings to others. This includes friends and family, church members, clergy, bereavement support groups, family physicians, or professional counselors.

Express your feelings in creative ways. For example, keep a journal detailing how you feel or draw or paint pictures.

Avoid negative behavior that can harm your health. For example, do not try and numb your pain by abusing alcohol and prescription drugs.

Set a small exercise goal each day. "Today, I will get out of bed and walk around the block once." Studies show that aerobic exercise significantly alleviates the symptoms of depression.

Plan ahead for grief "triggers." Holidays, anniversaries, birthdays, and other special dates and events reawaken memories and feelings. It is entirely normal for you to revisit your grief during these times. If a significant date or event is approaching, anticipate that you will struggle emotionally. Ask your family and friends for support beforehand, and work with them to create strategies to help you cope during this season.

IMPORTANT: We recommend you see a mental health physician (psychiatrist) if the pain of your loss is so constant and severe that it keeps you from resuming your life or if you have suicidal thoughts. Only a medical doctor can appropriately diagnose and treat grief and depression that is beyond what is considered "normal," referred to as complicated grief and clinical depression.[50]

---

[50] "5 Stages of Grief."

CHAPTER 15

Sixth Stage—Acceptance

If you have not resolved your grief, it will
affect your future relationships, including
the one you have with yourself.

—Unknown

The *acceptance* stage of grief is the final stage of the grieving and loss process. In this stage, the person comes to terms with the loss and can move on. It is about accepting the reality that the person's loved one is no longer part of the relationship. It doesn't necessarily mean that everything is fine or that they are no longer grieving; instead, they have learned to live with the reality of their loss. There is a gradual acceptance of life's configuration and a feeling of future possibilities.

Not everyone reaches an acceptance stage.

During this stage, a person may feel a sense of peace and acceptance about the loss. They may also feel a sense of closure and be able to remember the person without feeling overwhelmed by various emotions.

It is important to note that the acceptance stage does not mean that a person is no longer grieving. Grief is a natural and ongoing process, and a person may continue to experience feelings of sadness and loneliness and may, at times, have a longing for the person they lost. However, these feelings become less intense and more manageable in the acceptance stage.

It is also vital to note that not everyone experiences the acceptance stage in the same way or at the same time. Grief and loss are highly personal experiences, and everyone handles them differently. Some people may reach the acceptance stage relatively quickly, while others may take longer.

Getting to this stage is essential to move forward after losing a loved one, ending a significant relationship, or even receiving a difficult diagnosis. Acceptance isn't about moving on, nor is it the endpoint of the grieving process. Acceptance is about making new connections and relationships, listening to our needs, or simply living again—but only after we have grieved.

> It is important to note that the acceptance stage does not mean that a person is no longer grieving.

Remember, everyone can grieve in unique and personal ways. There is no right or wrong way to grieve or a specific time frame for the grief stages. However, universal emotions arise during the acceptance stage of grief, like hope and relief and perhaps moments of happiness. Acceptance does not mean you are okay with losing a loved one or relationship; instead, it is about rebuilding your life and living with the emotional pain of your loss.[51] Be patient with yourself because you must reach the acceptance stage of grief in your own time.

The process of acceptance could require some time before you fully attain it.

---

[51] "The Acceptance Stage of Grief: Characteristics and Coping," Verywell Mind, https://www.verywellmind.com/the-acceptance-stage-of-grief-characteristics-and-coping-5295854.

CHARACTERISTICS OF THE
ACCEPTANCE STAGE OF GRIEF[52]

These are some of the characteristics of the acceptance stage of grief according to Dr. Gundle:

- feeling positive and hopeful
- seeking out new meaning
- feeling more secure and relaxed
- engaging with reality as it is rather than what you thought it would be
- being more mindful and present
- coping and adapting to the circumstances
- being able to tolerate emotions and be vulnerable
- communicating in an honest, assertive, and open manner
- taking care of yourself and having self-compassion

FINAL THOUGHTS[53]

The time it takes to move through these stages depends on the nature of the loss, the grieving individual, and the overall circumstances of the individual's life. However, the vital thing to remember is that grieving happens in stages. Being stuck in one stage and dwelling on the loss too long may require the intervention of a professional counselor.

Sharing grief with those close to us is important for moving through the grieving process. But sometimes, it is difficult for others to relate to the depth of a person's pain if death is not involved, such as losing a relationship. This is our human nature.

---

[52] "Acceptance Stage of Grief."

[53] "Moving toward Acceptance," Sutter Health, https://www.sutterhealth.org/ for-employees/employee-assistance-program/understanding-grief.

If you or a loved one is struggling with the many challenges of grief and loss, we strongly encourage you to seek professional counseling with a knowledgeable and experienced therapist.

CHAPTER 16

Grief and Loss Therapy Types

Just because no one else can heal or do
your inner work for you doesn't mean you
can, should, or need to do it alone.

—Lisa Olivera

ART THERAPY

Creating or connecting with art can be a healing experience for many people. You may find relief in creating art on your own or consider working with a therapist specializing in art therapy. You could also consider connecting with other people's art if that brings comfort or relief.

The following are some art therapy activities:

- coloring
- dance
- decorating
- gardening
- music
- painting

- photography
- singing
- writing

ACCEPTANCE AND COMMITMENT THERAPY

Acceptance and commitment therapy (ACT) is one of the recent mindfulness-based behavior therapies shown to be effective with diverse clinical conditions.[54] The focus is to help patients behave more consistently with their values and apply mindfulness and acceptance skills to their responses to uncontrollable experiences.

COGNITIVE BEHAVIORAL THERAPY (CBT)

For over fifty years, cognitive behavioral therapy (CBT) has become an effective psychosocial treatment for many emotional and behavioral challenges.[55] CBT for grief works by helping you become aware of your negative thought patterns, and these patterns can lead to behaviors that make it challenging to process grief. During CBT sessions, the therapist often asks you to discuss your thoughts or feelings about your grief.

Cognitive therapy focuses mainly on thought patterns as responsible for negative emotional and behavioral patterns. From the perspective of cognitive therapy, negative emotional states are caused and maintained by ineffective or exaggerated biases in thinking. The critical intervention in cognitive therapy is identifying distorted or self-defeating patterns and learning to respond to them with more balanced, reality-based thinking. This results in fewer emotional

---

[54] R. Harris, "Embracing Your Demons: An Overview of Acceptance and Commitment Therapy," *Psychotherapy in Australia* 12, no. 4 (2006): 70–6, https://search.informit.org/doi/10.3316/informit.545561433272993.

[55] *Handbook of Brief Cognitive Behaviour Therapy*, eds. Frank W. Bond and Windy Dryden (John Wiley & Sons Ltd, 2002).

problems and more successful behavioral patterns. This process is also known as cognitive restructuring.[56]

Cognitive Behavioral Therapy—Rational Emotive Behavior (CBT-REBT)

REBT is a type of CBT that focuses on changing irrational thoughts or beliefs that negatively affect a person's emotions or behaviors. Utilizing this type of therapy, the therapist will often challenge or dispute irrational thoughts to help a person understand how they can change their thinking about events that occur. The idea is that once a person has challenged the belief, they can avoid unwanted or negative consequences.[57]

In a 2017 review, researchers analyzed fifty years' worth of studies and metadata about REBT. They conclude that REBT provides a valid intervention for people by helping them restructure how they respond to events.[58]

Complicated Grief Therapy

Complicated grief therapy (CGT) is a newer psychotherapy model designed to address symptoms of complicated grief. Drawn from attachment theory and rooted in interpersonal therapy (IPT) and cognitive behavioral therapy, CGT includes techniques like prolonged exposure (repeatedly telling the story of the death) and *in vivo* exposure activities. The treatment also involves focusing on personal goals and relationships.[59]

If you're unable to move through these stages more than a year after the death of a loved one or as the result of a divorce, you may

[56] https://cogbtherapy.com/define-cognitive-behavioral-therapy.
[57] https://www.medicalnewstoday.com/.
[58] https://www.medicalnewstoday.com/.
[59] https://doi.org/10.31887/DCNS.2012.14.2/jwetherell.

have complicated grief. Seeking professional help can help you come to terms with your loss and reclaim a sense of acceptance and peace.

GRIEF THERAPY

This form of therapy can help address your behavioral and physical problems in the aftermath of a loss. It can also help if you cannot separate yourself emotionally from the person who is no longer present in your life.

Grief counseling can help you identify and express your emotions. If you have lost someone who was integral to your life, grief counseling can also help you rebuild your routine and identity.

GROUP THERAPY

Group therapy remains a popular treatment format for individuals experiencing grief and loss. Group therapy provides participants with a peer-to-peer learning experience about the grieving process, which helps you and others form a bridge to the future.

Group participants share their thoughts and feelings about their grief and loss. Groups are designed to be safe and confidential, providing a nurturing and loving environment to foster healing. It is well-known that grief is often lessened when it expands into a social experience.

Furthermore, participation provides an opportunity for social support from other grieved individuals who can relate to the struggles of one's loss. Group therapy helps a person who has suffered the loss of a significant relationship, whether a parent, sibling, spouse, child, or other close relative or friend.

MINDFULNESS-BASED THERAPY

Mindfulness-based therapy is one of the newest additions to cognitive behavioral therapy. Mindfulness is a meditation technique in Theravada Buddhism that directs attention to the task at hand in a focused, nonjudgmental fashion. Although it is a cognitive intervention in some ways, mindfulness differs from traditional cognitive therapy in that mindfulness emphasizes sustained attention to the present. In contrast, conventional cognitive therapy relies more on Socratic questioning of assumptions about the past, present, and future.[60]

---

[60] *Cognitive Behaviour Therapy.*

AUTHOR REFLECTIONS

MELISSA ROBERTS

I began writing this book twenty-three years ago while working with one of my therapists who initially started this healing journey. At that point, I could write about the trauma in my childhood and young adult years, but I quickly discovered I could not go any further since my marriage was beginning to crumble. In addition, I had no idea how the story would end. So the book sat on a shelf for about twenty-two years, waiting to be finished.

After my marriage to Charles, I knew God wanted me to finish my story, but I still worked full-time at an elementary school. I retired three months later because I did not want to compromise Charles's health with his immunodeficiency. I then had the time to finish the story but kept procrastinating in picking it back up, even though I felt God nudging me to get started. That is, until John asked if I would coauthor a book with him telling my entire story. I knew, then, that God was opening the door wide for me to finish this unsettling in my heart.

No words can describe how therapeutic this has been, even though parts of it were difficult to write about. It is never fun to relive those traumatic moments of our lives. But I could see how God has protected me over and over. Writing my story also showed me how God guided me and provided me the strength to journey down that healing path.

It also showed me how far I have come through the seven years of therapy with John. Despite all the trauma I have experienced, I would not give up what I have been through because it has shaped me into who I am today. It also has thrown me into the arms of Jesus, for which I am so thankful.

I could not be where I am today without God's love, protection, and guidance. I see God's glory in my story, and I pray you, the reader, can see that also.

Don't give up on your healing if you struggle with triggers from a traumatic childhood or a marriage involving an addiction. I pray that my story can give you hope for strength and healing. But first, I strongly encourage you to seek a therapist who specializes in trauma. Some feel seeking counsel is a weakness, but I see it as a strength. Also, do not allow finances to be an issue. Even on my $19,000 annual income, God gave me the needed therapy, gas, and funds to drive the ninety miles to and from therapy. I had to address the financial issues and not give up hope.

Finally, I can only see myself making this journey with Jesus. He was my strength and stronghold when life felt hopeless. He helped me through my fears and broke through my firmly established barriers. If you do not have Jesus in your life, I challenge you to seek someone who is a Christian to discuss how you can ask him to be the Lord of your life.

Thank you for taking the time to read my story. I pray it was an encouragement to you. Please pass it on to someone who may feel broken as I did and desperately needs hope. I desire my story to inspire others to seek healing and live joyful lives with God as their strength.

Finally, I leave you with a verse that has had a tremendous impact on my healing journey:

> "For I know the plans I have for you,"
> says the Lord, "plans to prosper you and not to
> harm you, plans to give you hope and a future."
> (Jeremiah 29:11 NIV)

About the Author

John Sternfels is the owner and director of NorthPoint Professional Counseling Inc., located in Novi, Michigan. NorthPoint Professional Counseling is best known for its advanced counseling specialties in marriage, sexual addiction recovery, and partner betrayal trauma healing. John is also the author of *A Partner's Guide to Truth & Healing*, Amazon's number 1 best-selling book in the mental health category (October 2021).

John is a National Board-certified counselor (NCC). As a National Board-certified counselor, John is responsible for satisfying all educational and experiential requirements established by the NBCC Board of Directors and must demonstrate a past and ongoing professional commitment to the counseling profession.

John is also a trained LLPC supervisor. He monitors and assists limited licensed professional counselors (LLPC) to develop responsibility, skills, knowledge, attitudes, and adherence to ethical, legal, and regulatory standards in counseling. Supervision also provides teaching, coaching, and mentoring to the supervisee, respectful of the various levels of one's training and academic preparation.

John has facilitated numerous local and online workshops and seminars designed to improve relational intimacy, including *"Guardrails," "Helping Her Heal," "Collaborative Couples Workshop," "Cultivating Relational Intimacy Workshop,"* and *"Empathy & Intimacy Workshops."*

John is married to his wife, Kathy, of forty-seven years. They have three sons (Christopher, Jonathon, and Bryan) and five grandchildren (Cameron, Julian, Carter, Braylon, and Zoey). John and Kathy enjoy camping, hiking, skiing, snowshoeing, and spending time with their five grandchildren.

I want to thank Melissa Ann Roberts for allowing me the opportunity to be her therapist throughout the years of her healing. I am forever grateful that she agreed to co-write this book with me. My prayer is for this book to have a positive impact on the lives of its readers.

Over the seven years of therapy, Melissa was able to address her deeper wounds of the past. Allowing herself to explore and discover those deeper areas of woundedness, she now is experiencing perhaps the happiest times of her life. Yes, there were times when she was angry and frustrated toward me, herself, her husband, God, and many others. However, despite the many challenges, she clung to her conviction that the fight would be worthwhile.

Melissa found agency and acceptance after years of trauma and betrayal. She has spent over twenty years documenting her journey toward healing. She calls her story a "God story" and wants other victims of abuse to know that with faith and proper treatment, all things are possible.

With great admiration and respect, Melissa and I want you, the reader, to know that despite what you have/are experiencing, you can heal and reclaim your life. We urge you to allow God to do for you what you cannot do for yourself.

Printed in the USA
CPSIA information can be obtained
at www.ICGtesting.com
CBHW031932080824
12905CB00036B/648

9 798889 828525